THE UNKNOWN ODYSSEUS

THE UNKNOWN ODYSSEUS

Alternate Worlds in Homer's

ODYSSEY

Thomas Van Nortwick

University of Michigan Press • *Ann Arbor*

First paperback edition 2020
Copyright © by the University of Michigan 2009
All rights reserved

Published in the United States of America by the
University of Michigan Press
Printed and bound by CPI Group (UK) Ltd, Croydon, CR0 4YY

A CIP catalog record for this book is available from the British Library.

First published in paperback February 2020

Library of Congress Cataloging-in-Publication Data

Van Nortwick, Thomas, 1946–
    The unknown Odysseus : alternate worlds in Homer's Odyssey /
Thomas Van Nortwick.
        p.   cm.
    Includes bibliographical references and index.
    ISBN-13: 978-0-472-11673-7 (cloth : alk. paper)
    ISBN-10: 0-472-11673-8 (cloth : alk. paper)
        1. Homer. Odyssey.   2. Odysseus (Greek mythology) in literature.
    I. Title.
    PA4167.V36   2009
    883'.01—dc22   2008017340

ISBN: 978-0-472-03779-7 (pbk. : alk. paper)

FOR MARY
who has taught me the
meaning of *homophrosyne*

PREFACE

Who would dare to go nameless in so secure a universe?
Yet, to tell the truth, only the nameless are at home in it.

Thomas Merton

For the Greek hero, to be unsung is to be as good as dead. Nowhere does this equation seem to be more true than in the *Odyssey*, where a major theme is the equation of anonymity with nonexistence. Not only must Odysseus escape physical destruction on his way back from Troy; he must also avoid being permanently trapped in various kinds of namelessness that the poem portrays as death. This imperative is in keeping with the dominant perspective of the story. "Everybody knows" that Odysseus lives only to get back home to Ithaka. In the *Odyssey*, we see him first on the shore of Calypso's island, looking woefully to sea, longing to see his wife and family. So strong is his loyalty that not even a sexy goddess, with whom he has been sleeping—not always unwillingly—for seven years, can tempt him to forgo permanently the varied pleasures of conjugal union. And homecoming will restore him not only to the roles of king, husband, father, and son but to his identity in an existential sense. By killing the suitors he emerges from anonymity to become "Odysseus" again.

This is where the main plot of the poem aims the hero. The man himself, however, sometimes strays from the path. From his own mouth we hear that he went looking for trouble on the Cyclops' island and caused several of his men to be eaten by the monster, then insisted on sending a scouting party to Circe's lair, where the hapless men (Odysseus not among them) were turned into pigs. Neither detour was necessary for the trip home, and both led to disaster. Worse yet, once he'd defeated the witch with the help of Hermes' magic drug, he dallied with her for a year before his men convinced him to start again for home. These are not the acts of a man possessed by only one aim in life.

Things get yet more complicated when we note that in order to regain his full identity in Ithaka Odysseus literally becomes "nobody" and assumes various false, contingent identities and that in order to reemerge as the noble king whose spotless character contrasts so markedly with the duplicitous louts besieging Penelope he lies incessantly to friend and foe. Much recent commentary on the *Odyssey* by classical scholars, in particular the work of Murnaghan, Peradotto, and Felson, has focused on the ways in which the poem accommodates this rogue hero and, by extension, two different visions of human experience.[1] Peradotto, working from the Russian theorist Bahktin, calls the two visions "centripetal" and "centrifugal," the "center" in this formulation representing the goal of forces in a language or culture that exert a unifying, homogenizing, and hierarchical influence.[2] Finally the *Odyssey* seems to tame the urges to flee the respectable center. Odysseus comes home, reveals himself, kills the suitors, and presumably lives out his life in settled marital bliss. Doing so, he reinforces the firm identity, fueled by fame, that only being at home can—in the poem's dominant perspective—ensure. He is now safe from the annihilating forces of permanent namelessness; his contingent identities are safely put aside.

Apparently not all who heard the story found the domestic version of Odysseus believable since most of the sequels we know about in the epic tradition of ancient literature have the hero setting out for more adventuring.[3] It is as if Homer created a character who was too complex and unpredictable for the story: we find it hard to believe that he'd really be satisfied with Ithaka. He is, as has been said recently of another leader, a hard dog to keep on the porch.

The subversive, centrifugal aspects of Odysseus' character take us into the deeper implications of both namelessness and a shifting identity. While withholding his name and assuming disguises gives Odysseus immediate tactical leverage in various venues throughout the poem—he knows more about others than they do about him, and knowledge is power in the *Odyssey*—anonymity and disguise are also often the way of the trickster, the wandering, homeless figure who can gain entrance to the closely guarded precincts of the powerful. Relying on duplicity and generally unheroic behavior, the trickster can, as Lewis Hyde has lately reminded us, pierce through the permeable places in the membrane of established structures to a wider plenitude of existence that remains otherwise hidden to us.[4] Certainly Odysseus is akin to the trickster when he gains entrance to his own home disguised as an aged beggar. The further question would be whether his inhabiting of that role serves to open up the world of the poem in ways that would elude the more straightforward hero. To put it the other way around, what aspects of experience are excluded by the centripetal drive of the plot, and how does the poem acknowledge and—at least by implication—evaluate the loss?

As my title suggests, the two perspectives I trace are linked to Odysseus' return to his former status in Ithaka and, by implication, to his full identity as king, husband, father, and son. As he labors across the Mediterranean, his adventures repeatedly have him arriving at a new place as a nameless stranger, working his way to a more secure position, and then revealing his name in a triumphant reaffirmation of his heroic identity. Each cycle builds toward the final crescendo in Ithaka. Along the way, Odysseus' divine protector, Athena, orchestrates his progress, sometimes in ways that the poet likens to an artist creating a masterpiece. Athena's agency is only one of many examples in the *Odyssey* of artistic creativity, the most common being, of course, storytelling. In this sense, the return of Odysseus can also be seen as the making—or remaking—of Odysseus, through his own efforts and the interventions of Athena, beginning with his captivity in Calypso's oblivion and ending with his return to power in Ithaka.

The story of Odysseus' heroic return is also a story about the remaking of a particular heroic world in Ithaka. To live in this world is, as we will see, to inhabit a kind of fairy tale. But not all the characters in the *Odyssey* fit comfortably into this world. The most prominent misfit is, in fact, Odysseus himself when he assumes one of his various disguises. The disjunction can be discounted as long as we understand that the "real" Odysseus is never affected by the disguise but rather lurks undercover, manipulating others. But I will argue that the poet's insistent pointing to Athena's agency, in the context of other paradigms for artistic creation, urges a certain detachment in us from the imperatives of the fairy tale, opening our perspective to a wider range of human experience than the magic kingdom circumscribes. And with that detachment also comes an openness to the implications of Odysseus' alternate personae for our understanding of the account of human experience the poem creates.

To put it another way, the unmaking of Odysseus in his various non-heroic personae is also the making of a wider world. Most studies of the *Odyssey* have assumed that the heroic Odysseus is always the real Odysseus, that the world this hero, with Athena's help, creates in Ithaka is the only reality the poem recognizes. To read the *Odyssey* in this way is to put on Athena's blinders, to identify the poem with the fairy tale. To do so robs the story of its depth and complexity, its portrayal of human experience in all its untidy profundity. In what follows, I will begin with a reading of the poem that takes into account the perspectives of the centripetal return story—the making of Odysseus—and then turn to the other vision implied by Odysseus in his various centrifugal personae—the unmaking of the hero as the making of a new world.

I began to think about alternate worlds in the *Odyssey* in an attempt to account for what seemed to me to be a problem about the poem. On the one hand, its power to engage the imagination of subsequent readers and writers is as great as any work surviving classical antiquity. At the same time, I have always thought that the return story in itself—alluring and satisfying as it is in many ways—somehow lacked the requisite complexity and richness to account for the poem's enduring power. Rooting for Odysseus as he struggles toward home, thrilling to his crafty triumphs over monsters and distracting women, savoring the delicious ironies generated by his passage in Ithaka from homeless beggar to victorious king, all these are pleasures not to be discounted lightly. But still, I missed something analogous to the challenging brilliance of Homer's disturbing portrait of Achilles, or Sophocles' of Oedipus, in his prime and as an old man.

The recent scholarship I have mentioned, which uses poststructuralist theory to explore the implications of other possible personae for Odysseus and other perspectives on the world through which he passes, has opened up my thinking about the narrative form of the *Odyssey* and the nature of its hero. As the works cited in endnotes and bibliography here attest, there has been a steady flow of classical scholarship exploring these new ways of seeing the poem. At the same time, I have not seen many books that attempt to bring these perspectives—in a detailed interpretation—to a wider, less specialized audience. While I hope that my ideas are of interest to specialists, my aim is to engage readers of literature who may not be as familiar as professional classicists with contemporary trends in literary scholarship. For this reason I spend more time retelling the story than would be necessary for specialists, and I do not try to account for my reading by explicit reference to any particular theoretical paradigm or paradigms. Those familiar with these latter approaches will recognize the influence of audience-oriented criticism and postmodern models for a constructed self, as well as anthropological perspectives from folklore studies, especially of the trickster figure, and a view of character that reflects Jungian models. Translations from the *Odyssey* and other texts are my own unless otherwise indicated.

ACKNOWLEDGMENTS

I began writing this book during a research leave granted by Oberlin College in 1999–2000 and continued my work during the fall semester of 2001 when I was James Doliver Visiting Professor of Humanities at the University of Puget Sound. I am grateful to both institutions for their support. Special thanks are due to Molly Pasco-Pranger and Robert Garrett, my colleagues at Puget Sound, for their companionship and support during that lovely interlude in the Northwest. The central thesis of the book formed the basis for lectures given in 2001 at the University of Puget Sound, the University of Victoria, and Stanford University. I am grateful to my classics colleagues at those institutions for the opportunity to try out my ideas.

Much of the material in the book has come out of my association with Oberlin College these past thirty-three years. Teaching the *Odyssey* in Greek and English to bright undergraduates there has been crucial to me in developing my ideas about the poem. I also owe a great debt to my colleagues in classics at Oberlin, with whom I have discussed and taught Homer over the years, Nathan Greenberg, James Helm, Kirk Ormand, Jennifer Lynn, Andrew Wilburn, and Benjamin Lee. Their insights are all over my work, and their friendship has been a source of joy in my life. Karen Barnes, Administrative Assistant of Classics, has helped me in countless ways for the past twenty-three years. Nothing I have published could have seen the light of day without her support.

My association with the University of Michigan Press has also been a pleasure. Christopher Hebert, the classics editor there, and Christine Byks-Jazayeri, his editorial assistant, have given me great advice and support throughout the process of bringing this book into print. I am also grateful to the two anonymous readers for the press whose thorough and insightful readings improved the book and saved me from many errors.

I owe a special debt of gratitude to my friend and colleague David Young, Longman Professor of English Emeritus at Oberlin, who read the entire manuscript and offered many excellent suggestions that have improved the final version of the book. His encouragement and support during the time I was revising the book this past year have been invaluable.

As always, my wife, Mary Kirtz Van Nortwick, has been an unwavering source of support and counsel. I have discussed most of the ideas for this book with her and am grateful for her unfailingly intelligent and sympathetic response. The book is dedicated to her with love and gratitude.

CONTENTS

Digital materials related to this title can be found on the Fulcrum platform via the following citable URL: https://doi.org/10.3998/mpub.330831

Part One

THE MAKING
OF ODYSSEUS

Chapter One

THE HERO EMERGES

"Odysseus" exists in the minds of modern readers as a finished character: we know all about him. But of course we are seeing the hero from the far end of a long tradition.[1] Any particular realization evolves as part of a larger fictive construct and in that sense exists only within that work. Although Odysseus' earliest appearance in Western literature is in the *Iliad,* and the portrait in the *Odyssey* can be understood against the background of that work,[2] the character we encounter in Homer's later epic is finally and primarily the creation of that poem.

The making of Odysseus in the *Odyssey* occurs on more than one level. He comes into being for us, like any fictional character, as we look on from outside the frame of the story. At the same time, he also becomes himself *within* the frame of the story, reappearing after a long absence. He has been, of course, "Odysseus" at Troy, doing all the things that establish and guarantee his identity as a warrior. This persona draws on the Odysseus of the *Iliad,* and we also hear something about it from Nestor, Menelaus, and Helen. But the *Odyssey* is not a war poem. The centripetal hero of its story must be a different version of Odysseus, one whose identity is grounded in Ithaka. And because his return is problematical, so is his identity: he does not become himself again, in the fullest sense, until he is home, reinhabiting the roles of king, husband, father, and son.

For all of these reasons, the making of Odysseus is fundamental to the meaning of the *Odyssey*.[3] As he comes into being on various levels, we may reflect on the terms of his existence, asking in particular what they can tell us about how the poem is articulated and how it reflects the riddles of human identity.

BOOK 1: ABSENCE

The *Odyssey* begins with its hero missing. Indeed, the first four books—and to some extent the first twenty-two books—are informed by the absence of Odysseus, with all the dire consequences this lacuna entails. The centripetal plot of the poem is driven from start to finish by the imperative to fill the void, political and familial, left by the king's departure to Troy from Ithaka twenty years before, either with his triumphant return or with the installing of one or more surrogates. The narrative is, in this sense, comic in form, shaped by the need for *restoration:* nothing in the story, human desire or human suffering, divine anger or even divine love, can override this primary impulse.

Who will restore order and how are the principal questions the poem dramatizes for us. And because the disorder has multiple dimensions, full or partial restoration might occur in various ways. Odysseus has left empty four crucial roles: king of Ithaka, husband to Penelope, father to Telemachus, and son to Laertes. Only the first two could be filled by anyone but Odysseus, and they are not necessarily compatible. Succeeding Odysseus as Penelope's husband would not automatically imply succession either to the kingship in Ithaka or the estates of the king.[4] What we are told seems to suggest that if Odysseus were to be given up for dead Penelope could return to the home of her father, who would marry her to another man (e.g., 1.291–92; 2.114–15; 16.74–77; 20.334–37). Telemachus, meanwhile, when he reaches manhood, would appear to be the obvious heir to his father's estate and the office of king, but could not serve as a new husband for his mother.

These distinctions are not brought before us as the story opens, perhaps because the original audience would be presumed to understand them without explanation. In any event, the poet blurs them early on: we learn by the end of book 4 (663–72) that the suitors are plotting to murder Telemachus, which would clear the way not only for Penelope's remarriage but also, presumably, for someone outside the royal family to seize Odysseus' wealth and office. As for Laertes, we may imagine what would be in store for him with both Odysseus and Telemachus dead.

Even before we learn of the nefarious intentions of the suitors toward Telemachus, the moral paradigms embedded in the story make it clear that none of them would be worthy to replace Odysseus as Penelope's husband. And while Telemachus' basic decency is established immediately, he is not yet ready to succeed his father as king. Although the complexity of the situation as we find it leaves open many possible resolutions for the disorder in Ithaka, and it serves the storyteller to keep these potential outcomes alive, we are made to feel strongly the necessity for only one denouement, the triumphant return of Odysseus.

To return, Odysseus must survive at any cost. For this task he appears admirably equipped. The proem (1.1–11) highlights his versatility (*polytropon,* 1.1),[5] intelligence, and self-control; he has wide experience, won through suffering, and has labored in vain to save his companions from death. The next hundred lines or so tell us much of what we need to know about his situation. He alone is still on his return journey, stranded on Calypso's island; all the rest of the Greeks have either made it home or died or—in the case of Agamemnon—both. Though alone in one sense, Odysseus is nevertheless a favorite of the gods—all except Poseidon, who holds a grudge against the hero for blinding his son, the Cyclops Polyphemus. Athena, his special protector, prevails on her father Zeus to let her send Hermes with orders for Calypso to release the hero.[6] She, meanwhile, will go to Ithaka and rouse Telemachus, Odysseus' son. He must confront the suitors who are besieging Penelope, then go to Pylos and Sparta to learn about his father's homecoming and win his own *kleos,* "fame." Athena arrives in Ithaka, disguised as "Mentes," to find Telemachus unable to control the loutish suitors, who feast and make merry at Odysseus' expense. Though impotent in his own home, the hero's son immediately takes the moral high ground by welcoming the stranger, offering rest and refreshment. Hospitality will be a major vehicle for displaying moral qualities in the poem, and the suitors' neglect of Mentes further blackens their collective character.[7]

By its focus on Telemachus in the midst of the suitors, this opening scene reflects the essence of what Odysseus' absence means for the story. Male authority is lacking in Ithaka, and the result is chaos on several levels: the kingdom, household, and wife of Odysseus are all in a state of rudderless disorder.[8] The suitors range over the palace unopposed. Telemachus complains ineffectually, certain that his father's bones are bleaching in the sun but unable himself to fill the void. Laertes, we will discover, is exiled to the country. When Penelope descends the stairs to object to the hard Phemius' rendition of a song about the homecoming of the Achaeans—it is too sad, she says, reminding her of her famous husband—Telemachus rebukes her and she withdraws in tears to her bedroom. Odysseus' wife has been reduced to ineffectual weeping by his absence.[9]

Before granting Odysseus' release, Zeus muses on the flawed nature of mortals and offers a significant paradigm by which we may keep our bearings in the story (1.32–43):

> Oh my, how mortals blame the gods!
> Their troubles come from us, they say. But they have
> pains beyond measure because of their own blind folly;
> look how Aegisthus, rash beyond measure,
> seduced the wife of Atreus' son, then killed *him*
> when he came home; and yet Aegisthus knew this meant death for
>   him,
> since we gave warning—sent Hermes the keen-sighted slayer
> of Argos—not to kill the man or take his wife.
> For retribution would come from Orestes, Agamemnon's son,
> whenever he would come of age and yearn for his homeland.
> With kind intention, Hermes told Aegisthus all this,
> but did not persuade him. Now he has paid the price.[10]

Here again we see how a lack of male authority causes chaos. Zeus attempts to step in for the missing king, but Aegisthus does not have the requisite self-control to keep away from Clytemnestra, acting *hyper moron,* "beyond proper measure." Agamemnon's murder reflects the original failure of authority, which is corrected when Orestes is old enough to step in and restore order.

The story shapes what we know about Ithaka like a magnet passed over metal filings. Odysseus must return but with great caution. Telemachus, meanwhile, must be worthy of his father, ready to fill the vacuum in male authority if necessary. Beyond its immediate application to the family of Odysseus, the story of Aegisthus and Orestes points more generally to the crucial importance of self-control to the maintenance of right order.[11] Now we are in position to recognize the extent of the threat to Odysseus' return. He must guard against Poseidon and the suitors but also, perhaps, against his wife. His shipmates—whose failings are described with the same word that Zeus uses to characterize the failings of mortals generally, *atasthalian*, "blind follies"—are another potential liability: like Aegisthus, they are not able to control themselves and butcher the cattle of the sun; like Aegisthus, they pay for their lapse with death.[12] And finally we note that the journey home is going to be not only dangerous for Odysseus but also lonely.

PREVIEW: TELEMACHUS AND THE TELEMACHIA

The adventures of Telemachus in books 2–4 are necessary in order to get him ready to help his father.[13] Doing so requires two things: first, he must learn what he can about Odysseus, where and who he is, so that he can be ready to do his part if his father returns; second, he must grow up. The two tasks are interrelated in that Telemachus must learn about his father so as to have a model for his own maturation and he must grow up in order to complete the journey successfully. The necessity for change is, then, built into this part of the story. But the change that occurs must still function within the narrative's larger goal of restoring Odysseus to his former status. That is, Telemachus must change in order to help block change in Ithaka.[14] He must become ready to take over as head male in Ithaka so that he can make sure he doesn't have to do so. The paradox here comes to rich fruition in the contest of the bow in book 21. Telemachus is about to string the bow when Odysseus shakes his head. Telemachus then pretends to fail, and when the tension goes out of the bow we feel an analogous slackening in the plot, as father and son avert the generational collision that has been building since the beginning of the poem.[15] Odysseus "returns" to at least one of his definitive roles here, as father, and Telemachus enters into his inheritance as a son worthy of Odysseus.

In Pylos and Sparta, Telemachus encounters friends of his father who begin to tell both him and us more about Odysseus. From Nestor, he learns that Odysseus was unequaled among the Greeks in *metis*, "intelligence," and the master of *doloi*, "tricks" (3.120–22).[16] A boy as articulate as Telemachus could only be, vows the old man, the son of Odysseus, the great speaker. In this, Nestor avers with customary modesty, Odysseus and he were alike, and this was the basis for a close bond: never did they disagree in advising the Greeks in council (3.126–29). The picture of Odysseus from the first book is both confirmed and enlarged here. His intelligence, experience, and ability to persuade through speech are familiar. Now we learn that his intelligence can be used in the service of trickery, a morally slippery quality that might seem to complicate the original portrait. But for the moment, at least, Nestor's admiration and declaration of like-mindedness head off any qualms we might have.

At Sparta Odysseus reemerges yet further. He was, says Menelaus, the man the Spartan king loved most. When others inside the wooden horse (including Menelaus himself) were about to give in to desire and answer Helen's seductive voice, Odysseus held out and kept them silent (4.269–89).[17] Of the many tales she might tell of what Odysseus "endured" (*tlenai*), Helen remembers, with admiration and a certain fondness, his clandestine raid on Troy. Disfiguring himself and assuming the disguise of a beggar, he infiltrated the city unrecognized by all except Helen, who apparently overcame his cautious nature by bathing him, dressing him in better clothes, and swearing an oath of secrecy.[18] He told her about the Achaeans' plans, then slipped out of the city, killing Trojans along the way (4.242–58).

This prophetic episode reinforces again the implied approval of Odysseus' deceptions we have seen earlier. He will enter two more royal strongholds, on Scheria and Ithaka, before his journey ends, and in both he will bring suffering and death. In neither case are his secrecy and manipulation presented to us in anything but a positive light: he must do whatever he can to survive.

Menelaus goes on to tell the story of his confinement in Egypt and escape through the kind intervention of a nymph (4.351–592). Pinned onshore by the gods, he arouses pity in Eidothea, a sea nymph. Her father Proteus, she says, is a prophet who can tell him how to get home safely. On her instructions, he and three of his men ambush Proteus, who has the power to shift shapes at will, and by holding him fast force him to tell them what they want to know. There is much here that will also appear in Odysseus' trials: rescue by a friendly nymph, the necessity to overpower a monstrous "shepherd" by both trickery and force, prophecy of the hero's death far in the future.[19]

The import of these congruities for the portrait of Odysseus is significant. The episode once again marks with approval the use of deception and disguise in the service of getting the hero home safely. The nymph contrives a *dolon,* "trick," for her father (4.437): Menelaus and his men hide under sealskins to get close to Proteus; to mask the stench of the skins Eidothea rubs ambrosia under the men's noses. Menelaus' destiny, to live forever in the Elysian Fields, free from care amid the gentle breezes of the Zephyr, is contrasted pointedly with the plight of Odysseus.[20] Menelaus has been freed by a nymph; Calypso holds Odysseus captive. Menelaus will enjoy a godlike existence simply because he is the son-in-law of Zeus; Odysseus, noble and beloved by the gods, must suffer and struggle even to reach home.

This last contrast is part of a larger theme in the Telemachia, the continuing struggle of Odysseus when all of his fellow Greeks have moved on either to death or to a comfortable postwar existence. The stories told by Nestor, Menelaus, and Helen all have the effect of distancing us from the events they describe, as if we were viewing them through the wrong end of a telescope. For these people, the Trojan War is definitely over, something to look back at from a comfortable remove of time and space. The denatured quality of Menelaus' story of Helen and the wooden horse is especially marked. The king, now complacently regal, reminisces about his wife's former treacheries with amusement (4.274–89). Menelaus' apparent indifference can perhaps be ascribed to the fact that Helen has drugged the wine to mask the pain of remembering—the past may not be so distant after all. In any event, the need for anesthetization darkens our evaluation of the heroes in their new lives. They are not strong enough to face the pain of the war even buffered by time and circumstance. Odysseus, by contrast, fights on. For him, the war is not yet over.[21]

Because the values consistent with the urgency of Odysseus' return have been established in our minds by the poet, the comfort of Nestor, Menelaus, and Helen begins to look like complacency. Odysseus must keep moving, must fight against the forces that would strand him away from his proper place in the world. In this light, the future promised for Menelaus, which might seem to mark him out as especially worthy, appears somehow suspect, a kind of mindless oblivion. This perspective will be confirmed and strengthened in the next book by the Calypso episode.

At the end of his reminiscence, Menelaus effusively invites Telemachus to stay for ten more days at least. Eager now to be on his way home, Telemachus gently attempts to disengage. His speech, like much of what is said and done in the Telemachia, both previews what we will hear of his father and confirms that he himself has begun to come into his genetic inheritance.[22] He politely declines the horses Menelaus has given him, asking instead for a "keepsake." The land around Sparta is rich in fertile plains, he says, good for running horses, but Ithaka is too rocky to accommodate them. Still, poor though it be, Ithaka is the best of all places. This reply shows Menelaus that the boy is from "good blood" (4.594–611).

Like his son, Odysseus will win lavish gifts from those who admire him, and he too will put them aside the better to succeed in Ithaka. The preference for Ithaka over situations that would strike many as more inviting previews Odysseus' choices on Calypso's island and at Scheria. At the same time, Telemachus' behavior in Sparta shows that he is already becoming his father's son. In Pylos he announced his name and his agenda immediately; in Sparta he does not reveal his name or why he has come until Helen guesses who he is. His behavior at the court of Menelaus shows a skill in sizing others up and then saying just the right thing at the right time to get what he wants. Manipulating others by controlling knowledge is one of Odysseus' most powerful skills.

As we see Telemachus coming into being in these books, another crucial connection in the perspective of the centripetal plot, between fame and identity, is confirmed. Because status is conferred from without in the Homeric poems, a hero's identity is in part dependent on his being known by others. Odysseus' willingness to remain disguised and unknown is an important part of his endurance because by remaining hidden he risks a kind of existential annihilation.[23] While learning about his father, Telemachus himself becomes known to the heroes and their families in Pylos and Sparta. He wins his own *kleos,* as Athena has said he must. And by doing so he begins to assume his own identity as a young man.

The themes of the Telemachia fit together in a rich mosaic: to help his father, Telemachus must become a man; to become a man, he must learn about his father and be recognized in the world; but by bringing Odysseus into our sight again through eliciting information from others he also begins to pull his father back into being out of the annihilating, anonymous death he imagines for Odysseus when we first meet him in book 1.[24]

The first four books have introduced the major characters and primary themes in the story while establishing the controlling centripetal perspective through which we are to view what happens. In particular the Agamemnon paradigm and the conventions of hospitality suggest how we are to judge the behavior of the principals. The family of Odysseus, with the exception of Laertes, have all appeared, and their dismal state has been dramatized. Odysseus himself we have seen through the eyes of those who love him and those who fear him. The portrait that has emerged at a distance is already rich: intelligent, resourceful, self-sufficient, and self-controlled, long-suffering and full of fierce endurance, he inspires admiration and love in his peers and family. Adept at disguise, he is willing to remain anonymous in order to survive the hostility of the gods and the vicissitudes of fortune. He excels at deceiving and manipulating others for his own advantage, but, although these qualities are viewed as morally questionable in other characters, such as the suitors, there is no hint of disapproval in any of his admirers.

At the end of book 4, we leave Telemachus in Sparta and return to Ithaka. The abruptness of the shift is striking (4.620–27):

> As these two spoke to each other,
> the banqueters entered the palace of the godlike king.
> They led in sheep; they carried in hearty wine;
> wives with their beautiful headbands sent food along with them.
> So they busied themselves with the feast in the great hall . . .
> Meanwhile the suitors amused themselves before the great hall of
>   Odysseus,
> throwing the discus and the long spears
> on the level playing field, arrogant at their ease.

The contrast between the Spartans, whose feasting honors guests in an appropriate way, and the suitors, uninvited guests who wantonly waste the substance of another's house, could hardly be more strongly marked. The poet continues to reinforce the negative picture of the suitors that begins in the poem's first scene. We will now see Penelope again briefly, weeping and worrying about her missing son, whom the suitors send out a party to ambush as the book ends. As we are about to meet Odysseus himself for the first time in the poem, we are reminded forcefully that he must survive to avenge such heinous behavior and restore proper order to Ithaka. This overriding imperative allows us to condemn the duplicity of the suitors against Telemachus while we only hope that Odysseus' deceptions succeed.

REEMERGENCE: CALYPSO

Book 5 returns us to Olympus, where the gods continue at their ease. Athena revisits her campaign to free Odysseus: what good has it done him to be a king and a "sweet" (*êpios*) father? He remains stranded in the hall of Calypso, suffering strong pains, held by force, unable to return to his fatherland. He has no ships, no companions, and now the suitors plot to kill his son (5.7–20).[25] Zeus' answer takes us inside the workings of the poem's divine machinery (5.22–27):

> My child, what word has escaped the barrier of your teeth?
> Haven't you yourself arranged this plan,
> that Odysseus would return to punish those men?
> Contrive to send Telemachus back—you can do it—
> so he arrives safely in his own fatherland,
> and the suitors struggle back to port.

This is somewhat bald, even in an ancient poem more self-conscious about its medium than most. The effect is difficult to gauge. We might feel a slackening of the poem's urgencies: after all, we now know that Odysseus and Telemachus are at least going to make it back to Ithaka safely, and it is further implied that Odysseus will successfully avenge himself on the suitors. But, like all such prophecies in Homeric epic, knowing the outcome in fact only creates new questions, new urgencies. How will all this happen? At what cost? What form will the revenge take?

The complacency of Zeus here also echoes that of the Spartan royal family: in the long view of the head male of the universe, Odysseus' safety is assured, just as is the fate of Menelaus. On the one hand, this parallel strengthens the feeling that Menelaus is extraordinarily fortunate: rich, famous, the husband of the most beautiful woman in the world, and guaranteed an eternally blissful existence after death. He seems to be living the closest thing to a divine life that is available to mortals. But the Calypso episode will call this evaluation into question, as Odysseus is offered essentially the same kind of future but turns it down.

At this point, if we are alive to the story's centripetal promptings, we do not, I think, question the necessity for vengeance on the suitors.[26] Although in other worlds, fictive or real, quandaries about the ethical underpinnings of revenge might complicate our vision, it is not so here. Everything in the portrait so far of Odysseus, his family, and the suitors seems to impel us toward a clear demarcation between good and bad characters. Odysseus and his family have suffered in spite of their considerable virtues, while the suitors' violations of hospitality, parasitical greed, and nasty secret plotting make them deserving of dire punishment.[27] The poet will revisit this arena of moral judgment later in the poem, but for now the issue seems to be settled.

This brief interlude on Olympus articulates the poem's larger structure in various ways. By pulling away from the intensities of the suitors' ambush plot, the poet varies the pace of the narrative and impels us to view the action from a longer perspective. Echoing the beginning of the poem forms a ring, characteristic of archaic Greek literature, around the Telemachia, and punctuates the shift in our vision from son to father, past to present. And the carefree, unchanging world of the gods now provides a backdrop for a vivid and somewhat poignant scene between Odysseus and Calypso. Using the gods as a foil is common in the *Iliad* but not in the *Odyssey,* where divinity is felt most often in the form of specific interventions, with localized impact, into particular scenes. Here the easy life of the gods plays a part in a complex tonality pervading the exchange between Odysseus and his affectionate captor.

To set the plan in motion, Zeus sends Hermes to Calypso with orders for the hero's release. Some details are now filled in: Odysseus will go via Scheria, where the Phaeacians will treat him like a god and return him to Ithaka laden with gifts. He will see his homeland and loved ones again (5.29–42). Although gods can move from place to place instantaneously, if it suits the poet's purposes, in this case the journey is described in some detail. Hermes ties on the magic sandals, takes up the wand that puts mortals to sleep or wakes them, and darts over the briny deep like a bird that dives into the sea for fish. He even grumbles to Calypso later about how far he had to come, a nice touch. Expansion signifies importance in Homeric poetry, and here we can see the poet taking pains to draw our attention to this particular intervention.[28] The same could be said of the beautiful description of Calypso's cave that follows: big things will happen there we feel.

Highlighting the transition between Olympus and Calypso's island also perhaps invites us to compare the two worlds bridged by the god's journey. Doing so will take us to the heart of a definitive and delicately nuanced scene. Hermes finds Calypso in her cave, singing and spinning wool. The fire is of cedar wood and releases a sweet fragrance. Outside, "teeming" woods of alder, poplar, and fragrant cypress, through which birds flit, and meadows thick with violets and parsley. At the cave's mouth are four springs "all in a row"; around the opening cluster grape vines, heavy with fruit (5.59–75). Nature here is fecund and at the same time subject to a kind of restraint that seems to emanate from the goddess and her magical voice. There is order but not human order.[29] When Calypso sings, we never know what form her music takes. Are there lyrics? A story? Her singing contrasts tellingly with the songs of bards such as Phemius, whose subject is usually the *klea andrôn*, the "famous deeds of men." While their art is always in the service of human memory, preserving the heroic deeds of the past that offer paradigms for the civilizing self-assertion of mortals, the power of her singing is aimed at exerting an extrahuman control over nature, creating a seductive venue in which men forget their mortality and its imperatives.[30]

Calypso occupies a liminal space in the cosmos of the poem.[31] She is divine but lives far from Olympus; she is in nature but not quite of it; she is female but powerful in ways that mortal women are not. The poet shows us Hermes making the long trip to her island in part to emphasize her separation from *both* mortals and the Olympians. Before entering, he himself, though a god, marvels at the cave and its surroundings: this place is uncanny even for him. Calypso greets him somewhat formally, almost as she would a stranger, even though gods recognize each other immediately.

Everything here signals both beauty and—in the masculine imagination of this poem and early Greek poetry generally—seductive danger. Weaving and singing are both activities associated with female wiles in this story.[32] As the fragrance of cedar wood wafts around her lair, the nymph sits on a shining chair and will offer her guest a cup of ambrosia. In early Greek poetry, the combination of fragrance, ambrosia, and shining cloth is always associated with trickery.[33] This is a decidedly *feminine* milieu, as the early Greeks understood gender: an enclosed, womblike cave set in a space articulated by natural growth; the boundaries of nature and culture, a crucial polarity in the Greeks' characterization of human experience generally and gender difference in particular, are blurred here: the springs are "all in a row," but they gush forth; the grape vines at the entrance to the cave soften the stone and also mask its contours; Calypso's power over nature is expressed through the senses, fragrance, physical beauty, and music in its nonnarrative, beguiling forms, not—as in the usual masculine paradigm—through strength or intellect.

But perhaps the most daunting aspect of Calypso's island, to the hero of this poem at least, is that it exists outside of time and change.[34] She offers to make him immortal and ageless so that he may enjoy the sensual pleasures of her company forever, but he only gazes sadly out to sea, day after day. Once she has acquiesced—grudgingly—to Zeus' order to release Odysseus, Calypso puts the issue plainly (5.203–13):

> Zeus-born son of Laertes, resourceful Odysseus,
> so you wish to return home right away, to your dear fatherland?
> Good luck then, and farewell! But if you only knew in your heart
> how many pains will fill you up before you reach home,
> you would stay here with me, guarding this house, and be
> immortal, even though you yearn to see your wife, for whom
> you pine continually, day after day . . . And yet surely I can claim
> to be no worse than she, in face or figure, since no human
> can vie with the immortals in beauty and form.

Here the goddess speaks for us in asking the obvious questions. Why would Odysseus yearn for his aging wife instead of staying with the beautiful nymph? Why would he embrace his own mortality when the goddess offers an existence outside of the ravages of time? He could become godlike, but chooses to remain a man.

Odysseus' choice confirms what we have learned about him so far while further refining the nature of his heroic mission. His self-control is reaffirmed: he has held out against the nymph's charms for seven years. At the same time, his determination to survive takes on new meaning in this charged context. Not only are the implications of his choice starkly outlined here, but they appear against the backdrop of the Telemachia. The life Calypso holds out to the hero might well be viewed, like the fate of Menelaus, as the pinnacle of human existence, an escape from death and old age in the company of a divine partner. But coming after the scenes in Ithaka, Pylos, and Sparta, her offer takes on a threatening quality: not only would she keep him from restoring order in Ithaka; she would also—true to her name, "I will cover up" in Greek—erase his fame, the source of identity.[35] Odysseus' perseverance, which conforms to the poem's centripetal narrative goal of restoration, is now recast as an existential choice: *kleos*, which can be won only in the world of death and change, over an anonymous oblivion of eternal pleasure.[36]

Everything about these scenes marks them as especially significant: the divine motivation for Hermes' mission, the elaborate description of the god's journey and Calypso's island, the sharp focus of Calypso's questions. Having our attention, the poet adds yet more emphasis through the delicate portrait of the nymph. Given the potentially sinister aspects of Calypso's power over Odysseus, his choice to brave the seas might easily have been made to seem much simpler. But the character we see emerging in her exchanges with both Hermes and Odysseus is unexpectedly sympathetic.[37] Confronted by the god and his blunt order, she responds with anger. Why must she give up Odysseus? Whenever goddesses take a mortal lover, the gods disapprove and try to separate them. He came to her battered by wind and wave, but "I loved him and nursed him; I kept telling him that I would make him immortal and ageless" (5.135–36).

Calypso here becomes accessible to us emotionally, as few other Homeric deities do, partly because we see her wanting something she cannot have—experiencing, in other words, the limitations of a mortal life. But it is more than simply frustrated desire that draws us to the nymph. Other goddesses are, after all, denied their wishes by Zeus in the Homeric poems. What makes us care about Calypso is that we are made to feel that her desires are for something important and worthwhile, and thus carry a kind of emotional authenticity, unlike the petulant demands of Hera or Aphrodite.

Though she can apparently force Odysseus to do her will, Calypso's exchanges with him show both admiration and affection. Acquiescing to Zeus' command, she goes to Odysseus and promises to send him home on a good boat with a fair wind. We know from her retort to Hermes that she is angry at having to give up her mortal lover, and so her gentleness with Odysseus is all the more striking (5.160–61): "Poor man, do not persist in grieving or waste your life away. I have already decided to send you back."

Now, finally, we hear the hero's voice. His tone shows not affection but anger and mistrust. He "bristles" at her approach. He doesn't trust her and will not sail until she swears an oath that she is not planning some other evil for him (5.173–79). This response is striking for many reasons. Odysseus risks provoking the goddess, whose help he must have to reach home. Coming as it does in response to the nymph's solicitude, and given the fact that he does not know that his release is assured, his retort might seem an expression of either recklessness or outright despair. This is not the smooth manipulator we might expect given what we have heard of him so far.

Calypso's forbearance in the face of this provocation increases our sense of her emotional attachment to the hero. She smiles, caresses him, and voices affectionate disbelief at his "roguish" behavior—the dynamic between the two here in fact foreshadows Odysseus' exchanges with Athena, the hero's most passionate advocate, in book 13 (13.287–351). She delivers a handsome oath by the gods and a declaration of her compassionate heart. The two return to her cave, where she serves him mortal food and her servants provide nectar and ambrosia for her. After their shared meal come her questions, which invite a judgment about her attractions as compared to Penelope's.

The poet has created an extraordinarily intimate portrait of the nymph. Calypso is the first of many "detaining women" to appear in the *Odyssey*, alluring creatures who would keep the hero from his appointed tasks.[38] In this, she foreshadows Nausicaa, Circe, the Sirens, even perhaps Penelope. And yet the potential dangers she poses to Odysseus are mitigated by her tenderness and vulnerability. Though she wants Odysseus, and has held him captive for seven years, the exchanges between them here show not an omnipotent deity manipulating her underling but a passionate lover who feels both pain and genuine bewilderment at her failure to win the hero's affections.

Odysseus' response to her questions carries heavy weight in the story. The existential implications of his choice could not, as we have seen, be more important for the development of his character in the poem. At the same time, Calypso's vulnerability puts great pressure on him to answer with care. Though she has been kind so far, she is a god, and Homeric divinities are notorious for their petulance. And even if we feel he is safe, Calypso's genuine attachment to him creates another kind of pressure, to answer in a way that is worthy of her affections. If she had been shown to us as merely a selfish goddess, any degree of duplicity that got him off the island would do. But Calypso has our sympathy, and the poet must take care not to have his hero appear to be a cad. Virgil's portrait of the painful parting of Aeneas and Dido in *Aeneid* 4 owes much to this scene, though the Roman hero does not, as usual, come off as well as his antecedent.

Odysseus's reply is brief but effective (5.215–24):

> Divine mistress, do not be angry with me. I myself
> know all of this well, that discreet Penelope is
> inferior to you in stature and beauty; she is mortal,
> after all, and you are immortal, ageless.
> But even so I long, I yearn every day to return
> and see the day of my homecoming.
> If some god wrecks my ship in the dark purple sea,
> I will bear it, having an enduring heart in my chest.
> For I have already suffered much in the wind and waves—
> bring on whatever is next!

Here is evidence of the great skill and tact we have heard so much about. There can be no explaining his choice to this goddess without offending her, and so Odysseus does not explain. He admits his behavior makes no sense from her point of view and passes quickly to his stubborn desire, ending with a defiant assertion of his will to survive. The words do contain for us, looking from outside the frame of the story, the key to understanding his choice. He must have what his life among other mortals offers, the world in which he creates himself through action, winning *kleos*. The poet gives Calypso no reply to the speech, and the exchange between hero and nymph ends with their retiring to bed to make love. Given what has preceded, we cannot see this final union as forced in any way. Indeed, the poet's beautifully modulated scene leads us to the conclusion that of all their nights together this is the least forced, the most tender. Odysseus has stated his preference as gently as he can, and we are left to imagine Calypso's feelings from her actions.

The mood of reconciliation continues the next morning as Odysseus and Calypso work together to build his boat. She supplies tools and shows him where to get wood; he builds the hull and decks. She returns with cloth; he makes the sails. The poet lingers over the details of this project, taking over thirty lines to describe Odysseus measuring, cutting, fitting. Such attention is not uncommon in Homeric epic, where everyday activities—preparing a meal, beaching a boat—often receive elaborate portraits.[39] But in this particular context, Odysseus' craftsmanship carries a special weight. What we see here is a paradigm of *civilizing* activity.[40] The hero appropriates natural elements to create an entirely human object. All the attention paid to how Odysseus constructs the boat emphasizes his reconfiguring the shapes and textures of trees and plants to fashion something artificial, the result of imposing human intelligence and order on nature. The boat is to be a vehicle for Odysseus' return to time and mortality, and its making symbolizes his rejection of Calypso's mysterious cosmos with its inhuman harmony of art and nature.

The Calypso episode has put Odysseus before us, realizing the composite portrait that was building throughout the first four books. Hermes, envoy from the head male of the universe, breaches the boundaries of the nymph's timeless, feminine space in which Odysseus has been in a kind of stasis for seven years. In the exchanges between the hero and his divine lover, the poet has established definitive links between Odysseus' mission and his identity in an existential sense. His choice to leave the nymph's island is also a choice to reenter the world of time and death, the only milieu in which his identity can be established and affirmed. By releasing the hero into time, Hermes continues the project, begun by Telemachus, of pulling Odysseus back into being. Stirring the memories of Nestor, Menelaus, and Helen activates Odysseus' *kleos*, which guarantees his continued existence.

ESCAPE

Having emerged from captivity, Odysseus attracts the attention of his chief male tormentor, Poseidon. The god attacks by hurling storms at the hero's boat, smashing it to pieces. Here we see another aspect of the existential system by which the hero's centripetal journey is organized, the link between order and memory.[41] By shattering the boat, Poseidon reverses the hero's imposing of human order on nature, throwing him back into the formless sea. The god "covers" (*kalypse*) land and sea with his storm (5.293), conjuring up the detaining nymph again and threatening Odysseus with the oblivion he had just managed to escape. Faced with an anonymous death at sea, he wishes he had died at Troy, where his comrades would have "spread [his] fame" (*kleos*, 5.311). A huge wave now snaps the mast and drives Odysseus underwater for a time. He struggles to reach the surface, but the cloak that Calypso gave him threatens to drag him under. The goddess's power to induce amorphous oblivion lingers, still pulling Odysseus into nothingness.

At this critical point, yet another nymph, Leukothea, the "White Goddess," intervenes. Taking pity on the hero, she gives him her veil and promises that it will keep him afloat until he reaches land (5.299–312). The gesture is significant. Veils in Homeric poetry are always associated with a woman's modesty or chastity.[42] To relinquish her veil in public could, on the one hand, be dangerous for a woman, exposing her to untoward advances. At the same time, the gesture could be seen as provocative, forward.[43] Leukothea would appear to have nothing to fear from a drowning mortal, and in the context of book 5, where we have seen the hero narrowly escape annihilation by one nymph whose power is explicitly associated with a gift of clothing, her generosity must carry an overtone of danger. Odysseus is characteristically cautious, as he was when Calypso offered to help him. He keeps the veil in reserve, only to be used if his ship is completely destroyed. Poseidon then finishes the job, leaving him clinging to a single spar. Odysseus throws Calypso's cloak into the sea and wraps himself in Leukothea's veil.

The White Goddess keeps her promise, and Odysseus eventually reaches the shores of Scheria. In retrospect, we can see her gesture as a voluntary capitulation to Odysseus' masculinity: by surrendering her modesty, she restores a kind of autonomy that Calypso took away. In this context, the fact that we are told that Leukothea once was a mortal girl named Ino is significant since she works for Odysseus' restoration to mortality. Indeed, Odysseus' exchange with this nymph is part of a thematically integrated episode, from the time Odysseus launches his boat until he is left to depend on the goddess's veil, which extends and enriches the representation of Odysseus reemerging from nothingness. As a vehicle to effect his escape from the timeless oblivion of Calypso's island, Odysseus builds his boat. Poseidon then destroys his fragile link to order, memory, and time, "covering" the world with a storm and plunging him into the shapeless sea. Calypso's hold on him continues, despite her promise to set him free, as her cloak pulls him down into the deep. Leukothea's gift then counterbalances Calypso's.

Odysseus' struggle to reach land after receiving the veil from Leukothea is punctuated by four more uses of *kalyptô*, a verb that is always charged with significance in book 5.[44] Having given Odysseus her veil, the nymph dives back into the sea where "a black wave covered her" (*kalypsen*, 5.353); Odysseus is hanging like an octopus to the rocks on the shore of Scheria when a huge wave flings him back to sea and covers him over (*kalypsen*, 5.535); Odysseus finally reaches shore, finds a snug place to sleep under two olive bushes, and covers himself (*kalypsato*, 5.491) with leaves; Athena then pours sleep over him, covering over his eyelids (*amphikalypsas*, 5.493). The first use of the verb completes the handing over of the veil: Leukothea must be "covered" when she relinquishes her veil, and the sea compensates for her loss of modesty. When the wave throws him back to sea and covers him over, "wretched Odysseus would then have been destroyed, against fate (*hyper moron*), if gray-eyed Athena had not given him wisdom" (5.436–37). Once again, oblivion is near.

The last two uses of *kalyptô* are part of the imagery of rebirth that marks this part of book 5, as if to balance the threat of annihilation. After Poseidon smashes his boat and death looms again, Athena calms the waves (5.365–87). Odysseus spots land in the distance (5.394–98):

> And, as when life, joyful to his children, returns to a
> father who has lain sick, oppressed by terrible pains,
> long wasting away while some hateful power abused him,
> such joy then when the gods release him from evil!
> So joy seized Odysseus when he saw land and woods.

The simile creates a curious double focus. Odysseus sees land and rejoices as a child who sees his father return to life. But Odysseus is also the one returning, and so, within the simile, it is as if he watches himself being reborn.[45] The moment recalls—and perhaps comments on—Telemachus' plaintive remark to "Mentes" in book 1 (216): "Never has anyone known his own creation."

The theme of rebirth continues when Odysseus reaches shore. The fight to gain land has nearly finished him (5.453–60):

> His knees and strong arms were limp, for the sea
> had beaten down his heart. His skin was all swollen,
> and seawater gushed from his mouth and nose.
> Speechless, out of breath, he lay faint, and a bitter
> weariness swept over him. But when he revived,
> and his life came back to him, then he let go of

the nymph's veil, releasing it into the river
that flowed out to sea.

Odysseus has finally escaped the power of the sea, the agent of annihilation in this passage, and can let go of his protective veil. It remains only for him to find a warm place to spend the night. He decides to sleep under two olive bushes, one wild, the other cultivated. His choice is significant in two ways: the olive is sacred to Athena, and her protection of the hero is realized here in a particularly intimate way; the fact that one bush is wild and one cultivated marks Odysseus' bed as transitional between nature and human culture, a small symbol of a much larger complex of themes in this book and the poem. That he now can "cover" himself (5.491) suggests some greater measure of autonomy for the hero. The gesture, in fact, is proleptic: Odysseus, having been rendered anonymous for seven years, will from now on be able to choose to be "covered" by disguise if it suits his purposes. And the image of the smoldering firebrand, with which the poet describes the slumbering hero, underscores the change in his situation.

Athena's final gesture of covering Odysseus' eyelids with sleep has a distinctly maternal resonance: like a newborn infant, he is tucked in for the night. Indeed, *amphikalypsas* (5.493) is the last word of the book, concluding Odysseus' escape with a gesture that echoes the source of his potential annihilation in a slightly ambiguous way: Calypso, too, wanted to put "Odysseus" to sleep, and sleep, after all, is the brother of death.

Through his interactions with Calypso, Poseidon, Leukothea, and Athena, we are introduced to the terms of Odysseus' existence in the centripetal perspective, how his identity is constructed and guaranteed. First of all, he must be *known* by others. Anything that diminishes his *kleos*, "fame," threatens his existence. Fame is maintained through memory, which exists in time and depends on order. Though certified by reference to natural rhythms, human time measures the linear and irreversible progression of mortal life and in this sense exists only within the framework of human culture. Both the world of the gods and the cycles of nature are outside of and existentially prior to human time. And because the Greeks characteristically divided experience according to gender, with the masculine being detached from nature and the feminine being part of it, or at least hovering on the margins, we are not surprised to find that women of all sorts can threaten Odysseus' *kleos*. Calypso is, then, doubly dangerous to Odysseus and provides a potent foil for the poet's definitive first portrait of the hero.

CONCLUSION

A tidy formulation. But in fact much of the power of the *Odyssey* as a work of art comes from the ambiguous relationship of both the plot of the story and the character of Odysseus to this set of assumptions. The inherent conflict between Telemachus' journey to manhood and his father's destined triumph in Ithaka is part of a larger set of tensions in the plot between linear and circular time. Odysseus, who carries the forward motion of the story, contains within himself and exhibits in his behavior fundamental contradictions that undermine that motion. And since Odysseus' identity is dependent on his arrival in Ithaka, these ambiguities also complicate our understanding of his character.

Chapter Two

ODYSSEUS AT WORK

Having brought him into being, the poet sends his creation back
into the world of time and change, where who he is will always be
at issue on more than one level. Odysseus faces death in a physical sense
many times, in the sea, in the cave of Polyphemus, amid the suitors. But
for our purposes here, it is the other kind of threat to his existence, of
being *made nothing* in some way analogous to what he faces with Calypso,
that is of particular interest.[1]

Book 6 begins a series of episodes, some lengthy, some brief, culmi-
nating in his reentrance into Ithaka; in each of these, Odysseus arrives in
a new society as a stranger. Circumstances and details vary, but the basic
dynamic of these episodes remains: Odysseus withholds his identity until
he chooses to reveal it, hoarding leverage in a world where knowledge is
power. In each place he encounters potential threats to his return, and
since his full restoration as "Odysseus" depends on that return, his identity is also at stake in each place.[2] In this sense, the entire poem is about
who Odysseus is at any given point. As he makes his way home, he moves
closer to being fully himself again, but what exactly it means to "be himself" is complicated by those tensions we have noted in the plot and his
character. In the articulation of this succession of episodes, we can see
another aspect of the tension between linear and circular movement in
the plot of the poem. Each "return" completes a cycle in which Odysseus
begins as "nobody" and ends as Odysseus. But from the perspective of

the return plot, with its relentless center-seeking momentum, he is not fully himself until the last cycle is complete in book 24.

PLOT AND IDENTITY

Another aspect of the shape of the *Odyssey*'s plot further complicates our apprehension of its hero's journey back to himself. Books 1–5 proceed temporally in a more or less linear way, bringing Odysseus back into being from his enforced oblivion with Calypso while simultaneously propelling Telemachus from mooning adolescence to the threshold of manhood. When Odysseus crawls onto the shore of Scheria at the beginning of book 6, he begins a new phase of his return. Now he has some greater degree of autonomy, able voluntarily to forsake his identity for self-protection. We will never again see him existentially erased as he was on Calypso's island, though he faces, or has faced, analogous threats in many forms. He is, with Athena's help, proof against all—or nearly all—of these forces.

But of course the story does not unfold in linear fashion after book 8. When Odysseus reveals himself to the Phaeacians and tells them of his adventures in books 9–12, we see him as he was—or as he says he was—before arriving at Calypso's island. It has often been said that through this flashback the poet shows us how Odysseus has changed over the course of his long journey.[3] His rash behavior while leaving the island of the Cyclops, his miscalculation, which results in the crew loosing the bag of winds, perhaps even his dalliance with Circe all show that he had not yet evolved into the peerless strategist we see among the Phaeacians and later on in Ithaka.[4]

Perhaps Odysseus can be seen in this way to have evolved into a more accomplished manipulator of the world around him as a result of his trials. This kind of development, however, is not the same thing as the kind of profound change in perspective on life that we see in the Achilles of the *Iliad*. The *Odyssey* needs what we have come to call a "comic" hero, one who remains detached from others and emotionally inaccessible. His treatment of Laertes in book 24, unmotivated by the compelling exigencies that require deceit earlier, only seems to underscore the fact that in terms of his emotional isolation Odysseus has not changed at all.

A further complication arises when we consider that Odysseus tells his story in books 9–12 with a view to getting something in particular from his hosts: a ride home.[5] Ought we trust Odysseus as a narrator? His record in the area of truth telling is not impressive elsewhere when he delivers false autobiographies to Athena, Eumaeus, and Penelope. But Homer does not overtly mark the autobiographical narratives in books 9–12 as false or even suspect, as he does elsewhere when he wants to make truthfulness an issue. Though we can see reasons why Odysseus might well shade the truth to suit his own agenda, the issues that this kind of narration would raise do not seem to be of interest to the poet in this instance.[6]

Books 9–12 might suggest, then, some development in the hero's strategic self-control. But as a part of the poem's great centripetal theme, Odysseus coming back to life in all the fullness of his character, the adventures do not feel strictly prior to what we see in books 6–8 or 13–24.[7] In terms of his emergence before us as we look on from without at him as a fictive character, he progresses steadily through the poem, surmounting each threat to his existence as it arises in the linear course of the narrative. Only when he sleeps with Penelope, then reunites with his father and son against the suitors, is he finally and fully "Odysseus" again.

THE PHAEACIANS AND BEYOND

The affirming of the terms of Odysseus' existence proceeds through the rest of the poem. Though much of the power and delight of the *Odyssey* resides in the enriching, by repetition and variation, of this process through each of the remaining episodes, we can trace its major outlines in the hero's encounter with the Phaeacians.[8] Odysseus begins at zero on Scheria. He has been reborn in the sea, arriving naked and alone on the beach. The metaphor of rebirth recurs in the womblike cave of the Cyclops, whence Odysseus and his men emerge after the monster suffers *odynêsi* (9.415), the word in Greek for "birth pains," and at his arrival in Ithaka, where he awakens after "sweet sleep . . . the closest thing to death" (13.79–80) has fallen over him. While he sleeps under the bushes on Scheria, Athena works to assure a friendly reception for him, as she did for Telemachus in Pylos and Sparta, as she does for him later in Ithaka.

Homer begins book 6 by introducing Nausicaa, one of his most charming creations.[9] As with Calypso and Penelope, here the poet complicates the hero's mission by making the detaining woman sympathetic. Her exchanges with her father, Alcinous, show a young, impressionable girl on the cusp of puberty torn between curiosity about boys and the desire to be a "good" girl (6.25–70). Her overtures to the naked stranger who emerges from the thicket are at once innocent and forward, friendly to Odysseus and also—because she is thinking about marriage—potentially threatening. When he first meets her, she is without her veil, she and her young servants having put them aside to play catch, and the exposure symbolizes the tensions within her between innocence and awakening sexuality. Like Calypso, Circe, and Penelope, she must be handled with great care. Odysseus must have her help if he is to keep moving toward home, but too strong an approach could backfire. His speech to her, like his answer to Calypso's question, is delicate and perfectly attuned to the necessities of the moment. He flatters her with gallant references to her beauty but, by comparing her to Artemis, avoids scaring her off with overtly sexual overtures (6.149–85).

Nausicaa responds with interest but behaves primly. She offers to have her maidservants bathe the brine-encrusted stranger, but Odysseus declines, saying it would be improper for young girls to see him naked. He will bathe himself (6.186–222). This restraint is proper and reasonable, but the decision also reflects other levels of meaning in the story. Being bathed by women makes a man vulnerable in the *Odyssey*. Water itself is "feminine" in the Greeks' gendered division of the world, amorphous, flowing across the clean boundaries that define things masculine.[10] Odysseus himself has, after all, just emerged from a primal baptism in the sea, where his carefully constructed artifact was smashed by the waves. At the same time, Nausicaa's innocent offer of a bath and clean clothes also both recalls for us Helen's treatment of the "beggar" Odysseus at Troy, which resulted in his revealing his secrets to her (4.252–56), and foreshadows his near miss with Eurykleia later in Ithaka.

It is not only Nausicaa who poses a threat to Odysseus.[11] When he awakens on the beach, his first words betray his anxiety (6.119–26):

Oh no! What sort of people are these, whose land I've reached?
Are they arrogant, fierce, and lacking in justice?
Or kind to strangers, with intelligence like the gods'?
That's the voice of girls wafting around me,

or nymphs, who haunt the steep summits of the mountains
and springs of rivers and the grassy meadows.
Am I near people who speak my language?
Come now, I'll try to see for myself.

Book 5 has established that the context within which Odysseus reclaims himself is crucial. The strange world of Calypso, ordered but not human, erased him, as the cave of the savage Polyphemus, with its carefully articulated spaces (9.216–33), threatens to do.[12] The first three lines of this speech also recur verbatim when the hero awakens on Ithaka (13.200–202). Here and on his own island, he looks for the civilized human milieu that his boat making called into being, however briefly.

The ensuing emphasis on *voice* is also significant. He hears the shouts of either girls or nymphs, and by linking them the poet points to the potential for danger in these alluring sounds, which *amphêlythe*, "surround," him. The phrase "speak my language" actually renders the Greek *audêentôn*, which means something like "voiced." The adjective is used in Homer especially of the power of female song as opposed to the bardic *klea andrôn* and is used to describe Calypso, Ino, and Circe (5.334; 10.136; 12.449).[13] One expression of both Calypso's and Circe's mysterious control over nature is, as we have seen, their magical singing. This power occurs in its most potent form, of course, in the Sirens: when Odysseus and his crew come within hearing range of these creatures, the wind disappears and they are becalmed (12.166–200).[14]

Before entering the royal house, Odysseus reconnoiters, marveling at the harbors and public meeting places of the Phaeacians (7.43–45). After getting further advice from Athena, who is disguised as a young girl, he looks in wonder at the palace itself, decorated with much gold and other works of art, and the orchards, which are always in bloom with pomegranates, pears, apples, and figs (7.79–132). His initial question about the inhabitants would seem to be answered in a positive way here: the Phaeacians appear to be highly civilized. And yet some details of the scene might well give us pause.[15] The highly decorated architecture of the palace recalls the royal home of Menelaus (cf. 4.45–46; 7.84–85), whose life the poet has portrayed as problematic in its complacent opulence. The presence of golden guard dogs, "immortal and ageless" (7.94), made by the god Hephaestus for King Alcinous, and golden statues of young men holding torches (7.100–102), mixes nature and art, animate and inanimate, in ways that might remind us of Calypso's mysterious liminal cosmos ruled by her magic voice.[16] Likewise the everblooming fertility of the orchards, watered by two springs, echoes the teeming woods and springs around Calypso's cave.

All of these details reinforce what we learn in other ways: that the Phaeacians are, if anything, overcivilized, not an optimal milieu for Odysseus, who defines himself through action against hostile forces. These people do not fight wars, do not even have any commerce with other cultures, having all they need close at hand. They are polar opposites of the Cyclopes, who are savage and uncivilized. Each presents to Odysseus a model of society within which he could not be "Odysseus."[17]

As Odysseus negotiates potentially annihilating forces, we see how he himself—or Athena, working as his agent—can also co-opt those forces for his own benefit. So when he emerges from bathing in the springs (6.229–35):

> Athena, born from Zeus, made him look
> taller and broader, and on his head she set
> hair curling like the blooms of hyacinth.
> As when some skilled man, whom Hephaestus and Athena
> taught every technique, pours gold over silver,
> and brings to perfection his graceful art,
> so she poured grace over his head and shoulders.

This is one kind of "disguise" that protects Odysseus. There will be another, less attractive—his deformation to beggar in Ithaka—but serving the same goal: to give Odysseus control over his own identity. So later, when he is walking into the town, Athena covers him with a mist (7.41–42), which only melts away once he is safely inside the palace of Alcinous. The motif recurs in a curious reversal in Ithaka, where Athena covers the island with a mist so Odysseus will not be recognized before she disguises him (13.193–94).

Odysseus also controls access to his identity through self-presentation. The "false tales" he uses in Ithaka are an obvious example, while the adventures in books 9–12 present a more difficult case. As we have said, whereas the poet clearly marks the later autobiographical narratives as fictions, there is nothing in the text that establishes either the truth or falsity of much of what Odysseus says about his journey from Troy to

Ogygia.[18] He is our only witness inside the story, and Homer is our only witness outside the story. We have seen Odysseus lie on many occasions, and the rhetoric of the poem urges us to accept these other falsehoods as necessary for his survival. If there were something to be gained for the hero to lie to his hosts in Scheria, we would expect the poet to tell us and make the mendacity an overt part of the narrative.

As a stranger, Odysseus faces the threat of existential annihilation. Without his *kleos,* he is nobody. At the same time, by voluntarily becoming "nobody," he can control access to himself in various ways. The societies he enters as a stranger have an analogously double-edged investment in bringing him out of anonymity.[19] Treating guests well is one of the measures of moral worth in the *Odyssey.* Generous hosts confer some status on anyone whom they welcome into their midst, however little they can discover about him: he at least now fills a role within human civilization, where *kleos* can be conferred and preserved. There is also some degree of protection for the society in welcoming guests properly. The gods, and particularly Zeus, look favorably on good hosts. And by bringing a stranger into their human order, they defuse some of the potential for harm in the freedom that anonymity can confer. Greek literature is full of stories about strangers who arrive in some town and bring with them death in some form.

THE SHAPE OF THE STORY

Odysseus is the first and perhaps most illustrious of such strangers. As many have pointed out, his very name means "trouble," derived in etymologies inside and outside the poem from the word *odynomai,* "to hate." His grandfather, himself notoriously troublesome, names him (19.406–9):[20]

> Daughter and son-in-law, give him the name I choose.
> I came here having been trouble (*odyssamenos*) for many,
> men and women across the nourishing earth.
> So I name him Odysseus.

For all the good things that others say about him, the essence of the heroic Odysseus as he appears in this poem is in the name.[21] Wherever he goes, pain will follow for someone else. The rhetoric of the return plot urges us to approve of—or at least accept—the pain as the price necessary to get the hero back to Ithaka and into his rightful status there. The stakes of this heroic venture are high: without Odysseus, the society of Ithaka disintegrates, falling prey to disorder and moral chaos.

The allure of such a story is strong. The *Odyssey* is in one sense the first cliffhanger. Will the hero survive the elements, the detaining women, the hostile god? Will his son be up to the job of supporting him? Can he kill all those suitors? And what about his wife? Will she hold out and be there to welcome him after the carnage? Disguises and lying, manipulation of loved ones, none of this worries us if we have given ourselves over to the story. The suitors must die! The companions were fools and deserved to perish! Sorry about the Phaeacians, who meant well, but if Odysseus doesn't get home then nothing can be set right. One of the pleasures of a story like this is the permission we give ourselves to live vicariously in a world where the good and bad people are easy to identify. The *Iliad* is, for instance, not such a story. The goals of its narrative are quite different from those of the *Odyssey*. As a tragic narrative, the *Iliad* endorses as its ruling imperative the acceptance of limit and in particular the limit of mortality. Finally, Achilles must accept that what is most important is not what separates him from other humans, speed, beauty, fighting strength, but what connects all mortals, the fact of death. There are no good people and bad people in the *Iliad,* only fallible mortals.[22]

The end of the *Odyssey* has always seemed unsatisfactory to some, and looking at the way the poem concludes takes us back to the tensions in the story that we have been tracing here.[23] The poem's opening scenes establish, as we have seen, certain imperatives: the vacuum in male authority in Ithaka must be filled so that order can be restored to the royal household and by implication the larger society on the island; though many remedies for the disorder are possible, the dominant rhetoric of the poem strongly supports the restoration of Odysseus to his former roles as king, husband, father, and son as the proper ending for the story; as Odysseus moves inexorably toward his destined return, we also see him restored to his former self, which can only be fully realized when he has regained his rightful status.

All of these imperatives would appear to be largely fulfilled by the end of book 23. By killing the suitors, Odysseus reassumes the role of male head of the household, filling the vacuum in authority. In the course of doing so, he has reestablished his relationship with

Telemachus and, in the contest of the bow, defused the potential power struggle between himself and his son for control in Ithaka. Finally, when he and Penelope go to bed, he has resumed his role as husband. It has often been suggested that the *Odyssey* ought properly to end with the royal couple in bed, that what follows is awkward and perhaps the work of a later poet, not the one who composed the previous twenty-three books.[24] While this may be right, the difficulties of the last book can also be understood as the result of the conflicting messages within the narrative about the shape of the story and the character of its hero.

Book 23 ends with the coming of dawn, signaling new action. Odysseus assures his wife that he will be busy in the future on cattle raids to replenish his herds, but first he must go to find his father; she, meanwhile, should wait quietly in her quarters since news of the suitors' deaths will be spreading fast (23.344–72). Odysseus has told Penelope that his trials will not be over until he fulfills the destiny revealed to him by Tiresias in Hades, that in order to have a peaceful death he must first travel so far from the sea that no one has even seen a boat and then make a sacrifice to Poseidon (11.119–37; 23.248–55). The prophet's instructions do not specify when this journey is to occur, but the implication is that he is to set out after he has put things in order in Ithaka. For the present, dramatic tension has inevitably slackened with the threat of the suitors removed. That the poem should continue is not unusual in Greek literature, where many works feature a dramatic climax followed by scenes that trace the implications of the action. So here book 24 begins with the suitors being led off to Hades, prompting the reappearance of the ghosts of both Achilles and Agamemnon, a brief recap of the suitors' fate (and Odysseus' glory), and one more application of the Orestes paradigm to the family of Odysseus (24.1–204). After a two-line transition, we return to Odysseus and his companions, who arrive at the humble orchards Laertes tends in his reduced state.

Now comes the famous and troubling (the pun is intentional) exchange between Odysseus and his father in which the son, rather than greeting his father immediately, tortures him further with another false tale, sending the old man into the dirt one more time, before revealing himself (24.315–17):

> So he spoke, and a black cloud of pain smothered Laertes;
> grabbing dark dirt in both hands, he poured it over
> his gray head, groaning deeply.

The cruelty of this deception is stunning, even for Odysseus—the use of *kalypse,* "smothered," is surely significant here: Odysseus nearly annihilates his father.[25] Withholding his name has been an important strategy for the hero when in the midst of strangers, but here it seems gratuitous. We could say that Odysseus is simply being especially cautious: perhaps the old man has sided with the suitors. But in fact we and he know that is not true. No, this torture is not necessary by any sane measure. The poet has, in fact, made a point of letting us listen in on Odysseus' inner debate (24.335–38):

> He pondered in his heart and mind, whether
> to kiss and embrace his father, and tell him
> everything, how he made it home to his fatherland,
> or to question him first, and test him.

We begin to see the problem with Odysseus' heroic character as it has been created and as it functions within this poem. From the Calypso episode on, he asserts himself—perhaps creates himself—in the face of potentially annihilating forces. So strong is the portrait that when the resistance is absent, as here, the character loses much of its justification. This dynamic is familiar to anyone who, like me, grew up with cowboy heroes: once the maiden is saved and the dastardly rustlers put out of commission, the hero must move on, ride into the sunset. We cannot imagine Shane taking the place of Bobby's father, settling down to work the ranch.[26]

But Odysseus cannot move on. The goal of the return plot, to restore order in Ithaka, has been achieved, and now its principal agent has returned to the status that, as we have been told throughout the story, guarantees his full identity. He has survived and reached what is, according to the plot, the center of his existence, joined with his wife in the bed in the middle of his palace, anchored by Athena's olive tree. Indeed, one justification for the reunion scene with Laertes—at least the fact of the meeting if not its peculiar character—is the need to certify Odysseus' return to the role of son. But that model of identity conflicts with the creation of the hero through the course of the poem so that now we cannot easily imagine him inhabiting the roles that are supposed to define him. The plot requires him to be fulfilled while at rest, but stasis has been defined as the enemy of his very existence.

To put it another way, the return plot, because it requires restoration, implies the need to deny the passage of time. And yet we know that

Odysseus, Penelope, and Laertes are twenty years older than they were when proper order last prevailed in Ithaka. Telemachus embodies that period of time concretely, and when he is about to string the bow he dramatizes the tensions in the story between time and timelessness. Penelope also symbolizes the conflict in various ways. Her weaving and unweaving of the shroud is an attempt to stop time, an impulse reflected on another level in her behavior before Odysseus returns disguised as a beggar.[27] She is represented as being in a frozen state, immobilized by grief, unable to act.[28] When she finally begins to emerge from her paralysis, to reenter time, her actions create both crisis and opportunity for Odysseus: she decides to choose a new husband and move beyond the old order.[29]

Of course on another level, Penelope, like Nausicaa, serves as a tool in the machinations of Athena, for whom the success of Odysseus is never in doubt. The goddess' manipulations represent an alternate view of the world from what we see through the eyes of mortals: timeless and magical, glimpsed fleetingly in the scenes on Olympus, where the entire adventure is a game, the outcome of which is assured.[30] We might say that the return plot and its imperatives reflect this magic, supernatural world, while the human characters, whose very existence is defined by time and change, operate in another milieu in which mortals grow old and die and sons replace their fathers. So Odysseus, when he reenters time after his stay with Calypso, is defined by forces that must be negated if his mission is to succeed.

The last scene of the poem reflects these contradictory impulses in the narrative. Odysseus and his supporters, including Telemachus, Laertes, and Athena in her disguise as Mentor, have begun to rout the relatives of the suitors when Athena halts the conflict (24.542–48):

> "Zeus-born son of Laertes, resourceful Odysseus,
> hold back, stop the leveling strife of war;
> do not risk angering the son of Kronos, far-seeing Zeus."
> Athena spoke, and he obeyed, rejoicing in his heart.
> And so Pallas Athena, daughter of aegis-bearing Zeus,
> established peace forever between the two sides,
> keeping the form and voice of Mentor.

Athena's intervention is in keeping with her role as divine orchestrator of Odysseus' triumphs in the poem. She is acting with the approval of

Zeus, whose words echo what he said to her when she came to beg for Odysseus' release from Ogygia (5.23–24 = 24.479–80):

> Haven't you yourself arranged this plan,
> that Odysseus would return to punish those men?

Athena launched Odysseus' return from oblivion, and now she steps in to squelch the last resistance to it. Here, as in book 5, the poet seems to point insistently at divine agency, as if to question the significance of the human actors. At the same time, this tone is consistent with the focus on artifice at various levels in the poem, in the stories told by various bards—including Odysseus—within the narrative. As we have seen, Athena is herself compared to an artist when she creates a bigger, more handsome version of Odysseus after his bath on the shores of Scheria (6.229–35). And since artists are the propagators of heroic *kleos,* the guarantor of identity in the poem, we might see in Athena's manipulations the suggestion that she is not only Odysseus' protector but his creator.[31]

We arrive at the nub of the problem. Because the Odysseus whom Athena creates, supported by Zeus, cannot easily exist alongside the existential hero we have come to know, the continuation of the story beyond the hero's arrival becomes problematic. If the centripetal Odysseus is to prevail, then the narrative probably ought to end in the bed. We could more easily leave him there and be content with the inherent contradictions in his character. Once he rises the morning after, the major imperatives of the story are quiet: in spite of the supposed threat to him from the families of the suitors, he is home and the rest of his life has begun. Perhaps that is why Homer chose to have Athena cut off the story abruptly: anywhere he ended it would seem arbitrary.

TWO VISIONS

Sheila Murnaghan has formulated the dichotomies we have been tracing here in a fruitful way:

> The story that the *Odyssey* tells of its hero's disguised return serves as a medium for holding two contrasting visions in suspense. One is a vision of the difficulties and limitations of human life. It is eloquently expressed by Odysseus when he is in disguise, especially in his warning to Amphinomous; it is embodied in the hardluck stories that

make up Odysseus' false tales and biography of Eumaeus; it is voiced by Penelope in her expressions of despair; and it is exemplified in the world of the *Telemachy,* a world of valued but also ordinary social rituals, in which excitement is found in stories of the past, and in which legendary heroes appear in a diminished light. The harshness of this vision is tempered by its celebration of the various means through which these hardships can be alleviated or contained: social institutions, the continuity of the generations, the adaptability of the human heart, the vicarious pleasures of song.

The other is a vision of all these realities as a form of disguise, as a screen masking the true story, which is the heroic tale of Odysseus' glorious return. It answers the realism of the first vision with fantasy and wish-fulfillment. The interplay of these two visions creates the *Odyssey's* peculiar texture, which is at once more realistic and more fantastic than that of the *Iliad.*[32]

The principal tensions, in the plot and the character of Odysseus, can be understood in the terms Murnaghan suggests. That is, the evolutionary impulses in the Telemachia and the character of Telemachus coincide with the Odysseus who creates himself through action, while the comic imperatives for restoration that militate against change coincide with the centripetal Odysseus, who returns to his former self as if having avoided the ravages of time and mortality.[33] The two visions may also inform the difference between the descriptions of Odysseus by Athena and those who await his return, Penelope, Eumaeus, and Eurykleia, and the man we observe emerging before us as he makes his way back. The former group sees him as sweet, loving, and generous, openly expressing his emotions (4.689–95; 5.7–12; 11.202–3; 14.61–67, 138, 146–47; 21.31–41). None of these qualities is anywhere evident in the poem's present or Odysseus' own recounting of his trials. Instead, there appears the hardest realization of the heroic male that we have in ancient literature, closed off from others and unrelenting in his manipulation of them for his own benefit. The central question of the narrative arises once again: who is the real Odysseus?

The polarities we have noted may also be understood in terms of gender. Restoration, seeking the center, denial of change are, according to the Greeks' characteristic division of experience, associated with the feminine in the poem, while restlessness, centrifugal movement, and change tend to be linked to the masculine. So we find Calypso, Circe, Nausicaa, and the Sirens holding Odysseus back from his mission, while Telemachus, Zeus, Hermes, and—in their own way—the suitors are agents of change. Athena, as we might expect, seems to be less easy to categorize. On the one hand, she is a powerful agent working for Odysseus' release from those forces that would hold him back. And yet her ultimate goal is to restore Odysseus to his former position in Ithaka.

We may press these distinctions further by noting that the entire Trojan expedition is in one sense a masculine project, pulling all the Greek men away from the "center" of their lives, their homes and families. At the same time, the motivation behind the war is to restore Helen to her proper place, and one dangerous aspect of women in the masculine imagination is that—although their characteristic impulse ought to be centripetal—they may "go bad" and wander, blurring boundaries.[34] Because women are considered to some degree as property by Greek males, attached to the household of a guardian male, they must be controlled. Like the Trojan expedition, the return of Odysseus ultimately serves both the feminine agenda of restoring the center and Odysseus' desire to resume control of Penelope, who comes dangerously close to wandering.

With these distinctions before us, we might look again at the scene that many consider the dramatic climax of the poem, the reunion of Odysseus and Penelope. Having killed the suitors, Odysseus waits in the hall, bloody and victorious. Eurykleia, meanwhile, awakens Penelope with the news that her husband has returned at last and killed the suitors. The queen is skeptical but agrees to bathe and come to see for herself. After the maid leaves, Penelope finds herself in a quandary: should she hang back and test her husband or run to him, take his hand, and kiss him (23.86–87)? These are precisely the terms of Odysseus' own ruminations when he confronts his father later (24.235–38), perhaps suggesting some degree of leverage for the queen in her coming meeting with the bloody stranger. She then goes down to the hall and, despite Telemachus' complaints, hangs back.[35] Odysseus reassures his son: he is hardly recognizable now, but his wife will come around in time. Meanwhile, he sets in motion a false wedding celebration to tamp down the suspicions of outsiders and retires to bathe.

Odysseus is bathed by Eurynome, a faithful maidservant. As he emerges, we are told that Athena makes him bigger and more handsome, her work here being compared in a simile to a master artisan who pours gold over silver. The language of the passage is, with the exception of one line, exactly the same as when the goddess augments the hero after he bathes himself on the beach at Scheria (6.229–35 = 23.156–62). We have seen that being bathed can be dangerous for a man in the *Odyssey*, but since the suitors are vanquished we may feel that the parallels here emphasize the difference in the hero's situation. Now he is finally home, and it is safe for him to be bathed.

And yet, what happens to Odysseus next? He returns to the hall in his glory, but Penelope still holds back. Complaining of her strange behavior, her hard heart, he testily orders that a bed be set up for him: he will sleep alone. To which, she replies that he is also "strange," in that he resembles Odysseus as he was twenty years before, when he sailed for Troy, and then gives the famous order to have their marriage bed moved out into the hallway. Now, finally, the great tactician loses control, revealing himself as Odysseus but not, as was the case in all other places where he has arrived as a stranger, on his own terms. Only one other woman ever succeeds in getting Odysseus to reveal himself: Helen. Coming upon him in disguise as a beggar, she questions him, but he keeps quiet until she bathes him, gives him fresh clothes, and swears not to reveal his identity to the Trojans. He then tells her all the Achaeans' plans (*Odyssey* 4.250–56). In this light, Penelope's later implied comparison of herself to Helen takes on added significance (23.218–24).[36]

Putting this final recognition scene in the context of analogous passages suggests, then, some further thought about the nature of Odysseus' homecoming. As she does when he is facing the challenge of negotiating Nausicaa's potential for snaring him as a husband and thus detaining him from his return, Athena makes Odysseus bigger and more attractive. Having been bathed and dressed, he then loses control of himself and reveals his identity on Penelope's terms. Because we know that Odysseus is "safe," the parallels between Penelope and various detaining women in the poem do not, perhaps, strike us as forcefully as they might if he were still dispossessed. Here, as always, the rhetoric of the return plot urges us to elevate centripetal imperatives above other forces in the story. Nevertheless, though muted, the suggestion persists that Odysseus, having arrived home and repossessed his former life, may have entered an arena that resembles in disturbing ways both Ogygia and Scheria.

THE IDENTITIES OF ODYSSEUS

We return to the question of Odysseus' identity. How the hero is presented to us is, as we have seen, governed by the interplay between two competing visions of human life. The articulation and significance of these two perspectives are complex and fraught with seeming difficulties for anyone attempting to define them. Murnaghan's useful formulation aligns the return of Odysseus—and the implication that various kinds of enduring "truth" are to be certified by that return—with a magical world governed to a large extent by divine powers beyond the reach of human control. Here the plan of Athena, revealed to us in divine assemblies, guarantees the hero's success and elevates that outcome to a level of importance that transcends any qualms we may have about the means by which Odysseus achieves his goal. In this view, the "real" Odysseus is revealed only in the aftermath of the bloody triumph of book 22 and verified by his position as king, husband, father, and son. All the personae we see beforehand, diminished by age and circumstance, are only disguised versions of the real man. This Odysseus exists beyond the reach of time, looking just like the young man who left for Troy (23.174–76); this Odysseus is kind, generous, and entirely deserving of complete loyalty from all who know him.

The other Odysseus comes into being before our eyes fully within the fragile world of time and change. His existence is defined for us in the Calypso episode, where he refuses what seems to be a version of the magical, timeless world of the gods, choosing instead to live out his life as a human, subject to the forces of time and mortality. He explicitly rejects immortality, the implication being that it represents for him oblivion, a milieu within which he might as well be dead because he cannot win *kleos* while stranded—however luxuriously—within Calypso's world. This version of Odysseus understands himself according to what we call an existential perspective. That is, in order to exist, he must express his identity through action in the world, creating himself through that action, a dynamic that informs the repeated cycles of death and rebirth that articulate Odysseus' progress from stranger to famous hero.

This latter Odysseus fits less well into Athena's centripetal agenda. The foray into the Cyclops' cave, the fact-finding mission to Circe's lair, the hero's listening to the Sirens are all motivated by a desire for knowledge, not by the immediate demands of the return home. The need to know, in turn, reflects Odysseus' desire to control his destiny: knowledge brings power in the *Odyssey*, the result of imposing intellectual structure on what is originally beyond human intellect. All of these latter urges are what we might call centrifugal, taking the hero away from the straight path to Ithaka and toward sources of knowledge and power that can be tapped through the hero's self-assertion rather than supplied by the intervention of the gods. We note here that in the *Iliad* there is drawn a firm distinction—particularly but not exclusively in the character of Achilles—between the winning of *kleos,* which requires staying in Troy, and the safe but unheroic longevity that would result from going home. Perhaps the Odysseus of the *Odyssey* is not so different from Achilles in the *Iliad* after all.

The collision of these two different versions of Odysseus in books 23 and 24 creates, as we have seen, the curiously problematic ending of the poem. Odysseus knows he is being helped by Athena, but he is nevertheless presented to us as a man who thinks he is making his own way through a perilous landscape, using all of his powers of deception and self-concealment to gain leverage over others. All the while, the goddess is hovering, implementing her plan, which is presented as irresistibly powerful and beyond dispute. When he defeats the suitors and wins back Penelope, the centripetal Odysseus is revealed to be his true self in all his various roles. But the centrifugal Odysseus, created by his own self-assertion in the face of the powers of oblivion, cannot exist in stasis, must always be making himself anew. While the centripetal Odysseus exists only insofar as the masks are off, the centrifugal version can only experience the marriage bed, anchored at the center of the house by Athena's olive tree, as the milieu of the detaining woman; while the centripetal Odysseus reaches fulfillment while at rest in his own home, the centrifugal version will always be adopting the role of stranger.

The presence of two alternate views of human life is not unique to the *Odyssey.* The final scenes between Achilles and Priam in the *Iliad* bring to fruition a perspective that contrasts starkly with the dominant view of the warrior ethic that pervades the rest of the poem. In the place of the hierarchical, competitive system of values found in the warrior society and embodied most vividly by Achilles, where status is dependent on being the swiftest, the tallest, the most beautiful, there is offered a view of human life—exemplified earlier by Patroclus—in which honor is given to accepting one's place in a larger scheme; humility, not self-assertion, characterizes the mature man in this perspective. Indeed, the ransoming of Hector represents the ascendancy, however fleeting, of this alternate view of life, an interlude before the resumption of fighting.

All that being said, the articulation of competing visions in the *Odyssey* is markedly different from that in the *Iliad.* The change in Achilles at the end of the poem is presented as a movement in him toward acknowledging parts of himself that his arrogance and pride have driven out of view: he will fight on after the truce but not, it is implied, with the same acceptance of the competitive values that motivated his earlier prowess.[37] Because he is the focal point through which the *Iliad's* picture of human life and death are presented, this transformation in Achilles also serves as the vehicle for a thematic synthesis that informs the entire poem and brings it to a satisfying if somber conclusion.

The two views of human life offered in the *Odyssey* do not function in the same way within the poem's structure. The centripetal, divinely orchestrated world that is restored at the end of the poem is not, as we have seen, the backdrop for a cleanly articulated thematic synthesis. Odysseus' character, as we have come to know it, fits uneasily into the cozy, settled cosmos of Ithaka after the suitors are killed. Instead, he represents a kind of subversive agent in the midst of his own supposed domestic bliss. Whereas we can understand both versions of Achilles—and the different views of human life they exemplify—within the world created in the *Iliad,* the magical Odysseus, unmarked by time and change—and the corresponding world of Ithaka, showing no effects from the twenty-year hiatus—cannot so easily coexist with the centrifugal, evolving hero we see struggling to make his way home. Likewise, the world of death and change within which this latter version of Odysseus moves cannot be reconciled with the magic kingdom.

CONCLUSION: CLOSED AND OPEN WORLDS

As Odysseus moves ever closer to triumphing over the suitors and restoring order in Ithaka, he is recognized by those who have not seen him for twenty years, Telemachus, Eumaeus, Argos, Eurykleia. Then, after the slaughter of the suitors, these recognitions come to fruition in the scenes with Penelope and Laertes, finally confirming the identity of the king. Restoration of the true Ithaka coincides with revelation of the true Odysseus. Insofar as we accept the centripetal rhetoric of the plot, these climactic events confer a sense of closure. We appreciate, from this perspective, the poet's skillful manipulation of our desire for reconciliation, teasing us with Penelope's uncertainty.

We want closure because we want things to make sense, to add up. To find meaning, as interpreters of literature or observers of the world around us, requires the discerning of patterns in the flux of experience. But, as we have seen, things in the *Odyssey* do not quite add up. The tensions in the plot and the character of Odysseus persist however much we would like a tidier structure. If we are to experience the full richness of Homer's poem as a work of art and a reflection of human life, we must also follow where the subversive, centrifugal elements in the narrative lead. Frank Kermode, referring to characters in James Joyce's *Ulysses,* puts it this way:

> We are all fulfillment men, *pleromatists;* we seek the center that will allow the senses to rest, at any rate for one interpreter, at any rate for one moment. If the text has a great many details that puzzle us, we ask where they popped up from. Our answers will be very diverse: Theoclymenos or Stanislaus, Mr. Duffy or Death, a hooded phallus haunting tombs, a mimesis of fortuity and therefore not in itself fortuitous. Or perhaps: a candidate for baptism; a lover; a mimesis of actuality; a signature. We halt the movement of the senses, or try to. Sometimes the effort is great. Bloom failed with the man in the macintosh; the hour was late, too late for him to sort out carnal and spiritual, manifest and latent, revealed or concealed. He had had a long hard day and went, quite carnally, to bed. Perhaps he returned to the question later, as we must.[38]

Part Two

THE UNMAKING
OF ODYSSEUS

Chapter Three

SUBVERSIVE ANONYMITY

My place is in reality no place, and I hesitate to act as if I were anything but a stranger anywhere . . . I am an alien and a transient, and this is the last happiness that is possible to me . . .

Thomas Merton

A nonymity carries a potent meaning in the *Odyssey*. To the hero intent on winning *kleos,* being nameless is the same as being dead. If the time for dying has come, then better always to leave this world in the presence of others, winning fame on the way out, than to disappear anonymously, smothered by some amorphous force. Then, at least, one lives on in heroic song. Yet because *kleos* can not only confer power but also prompt challenges to that power in the intensely competitive heroic world, to control access to one's own identity can create leverage in a new place: knowledge brings power in the *Odyssey,* and to be a stranger relieves one of the burdens and potential dangers of fame. Odysseus is the master of namelessness, and this expertise is crucial to understanding the centrifugal aspects of his character.

In this chapter and those that follow, we will be giving ourselves permission to detach somewhat from the imperatives of the return plot. As he makes his way across the seas toward home, Odysseus both embodies and encounters ways of being that lead away from the centripetal agenda, suggesting a wider perspective on the nature of human experience than is implied by the traditional heroic scale of values. Viewed through the lens of Athena's return plot, these ways of experiencing life look dangerous for Odysseus because if he followed out their implications he would not make it back to the goddess's olive tree, would not restore the world as it has been and should be, would not be the hero he must be. The dominant rhetoric of the poem urges us to accept Athena's view, to understand the centripetal aspects of the story and its hero as more genuine, reflecting how the world ought to be ordered. But the *Odyssey* has a richer understanding of the nature of human life than what is implied by the fairy-tale return plot. This richness comes into bloom through the poem's characteristic ironies, which are generated by the clash between centripetal and centrifugal perspectives. To hear these ironies, we must be attuned to both views; we must recognize that unmaking Odysseus opens the way to a more spacious world.

THE ARRIVAL OF THE STRANGER

The story begins in the shadow of evil done in the past. A stranger arrives in town, and death comes in his wake.[1] This pattern recurs frequently in Greek epic and dramatic literature: the *Iliad,* all the Orestes plays, *Oedipus Rex, Oedipus at Colonus, Medea, The Bacchae,* and many more are based on it.[2] The allure of the story is clear enough. First of all, there is displacement: the protagonist has left his customary venue and encounters new and perhaps strange people and situations. He, in turn, injects himself, as a source of the new and unfamiliar, into a tightly knit social group and creates by his presence a ripple in the fabric of others' lives. Since the entire sequence of events plays out against the background of earlier disturbances of right order, the effects of which are somehow still active, there is an air of apprehension and irresolution built into the story: something is out of joint, and the energy of the plot comes from the strains this warping creates. And because the unwinding of this dramatic spring brings death, the story confronts us with a definitive element in human life, mortality.

These elements are present not just in Greek literature but in the art of myriad cultures, ancient and modern. Both the typical American cowboy myth of the late nineteenth and early twentieth centuries and the *Epic of Gilgamesh,* much older than the *Iliad,* are shaped by the same sequence. That the pattern should be especially arresting to Greeks of the Archaic and classical periods is not surprising. The xenophobia common to Greek towns in antiquity, along with a curiosity about things new that characterizes ancient Greek intellectual life, would combine paradoxically to foster an intense interest in strangers and their effect on a close-knit society based on kinship ties. The *Odyssey* in particular seems to reflect the unsettled ninth century BCE, when Greek and other cultures around the Mediterranean were beginning to emerge from various kinds of political and social upheaval.[3] Wandering men and households in flux would be alluring topics in such a time.

The identity of the stranger is always integral to the working out of the plot: Who is he? Why is he here? A recognition scene provides a pivot around which the story turns, sometimes leading to the dramatic climax, sometimes being itself the climax. The audience always knows more than the characters in the story, so dramatic irony inevitably informs the plot. The supreme example of this particular dynamic is Sophocles' *Oedipus Rex*. There what we know as opposed to what Oedipus knows fills us with dread and primes us for the shattering climax occasioned by the play's recognition scene. We look on in horror as the king's relentless search for the truth leads to his own destruction. As Oedipus' true identity and history come slowly to light, we participate vicariously in the response first of Jocasta, then of Oedipus himself. Much of the power of the play comes from the tight economy of its plot: recognition and catastrophe are simultaneous; the hero moves from glory to ignominy in an instant.

Oedipus Rex also exemplifies a further plot twist that is fairly common: the stranger is not really a stranger but someone intimately connected to the society into which he has moved. The arrival eventually becomes a *nostos*, the stranger someone known. Because the stranger has been away, he brings change, perhaps reflecting a transformation in himself, which fosters further dislocation. Recognition, as we have seen, brings about a blending of the familiar and the new. Orestes, in Aeschylus' *Libation Bearers* and Sophocles' *Electra*, returns home a young man, having left as a boy. In Euripides' *Bacchae*, Dionysus, now a powerful and exotic god, reenters the city where he was conceived years before. Both sons bear a grudge; both bring death.

ODYSSEUS AS THE AGENT OF DEATH

These examples from tragedy offer in a compressed form what the *Odyssey* plays out repeatedly. As we have seen, Odysseus is a stranger in nearly every place where he arrives, even Ithaka. To each new place, he brings uncertainty, disorder, and pain. And in nearly every instance his arrival occasions death in some form. We might go so far as to say that Odysseus is the principal agent of mortality and change in the poem. Helen's reminiscence of his clandestine raid on Troy and subsequent leadership inside the lethal wooden horse extends that motif backward in time to the Trojan War. The thematic connections between that mission and his subsequent adventures on the way home suggest that in a sense Odysseus replays the fall of Troy all along the way home. Not for nothing does he identity himself to the blinded Cyclops as "Odysseus, Sacker of Cities" (10.530).

The interlude on Scheria provides a bridge between the entirely non-human world of Calypso's island and Ithaka. The Phaeacians are mortal but live a life divorced from the rigors of normal human existence. Living in Hyperia was too close to the Cyclopes, who represent the brutish end of the continuum of civilization, so Nausithous led them to Scheria, a remote island, where they put up walls, built houses and temples, and plowed fields (6.4–10). There they have no commerce with other societies, preferring to stay on their island, eschewing war, enjoying themselves by dancing, singing, and harmless athletics. We might also say that the Phaeacians represent a *mediated* encounter with human life. Their excellence lies in a kind of reinterpretation of the primary forces that impinge on mortals in the poem. They love games, structured experiences one level removed from ordinary human converse; instead of war, they compete in athletics.

Some aspects of this sort of existence are normally characterized as *soft,* perhaps a little too feminine, in the heroic perspective of Greek epic, the kind of life one might expect to find among the effeminate peoples of the east. To be sure, the world of the Phaeacians is less obviously feminized than Calypso's realm, but after his enforced stay on Ogygia, Odysseus might well feel some qualms about a society in which the key to his escape lies in the placating of two women, first Nausicaa, then Arete. He finally succeeds in winning them over, and in both cases, the conquests rehearse his encounter with Penelope in Ithaka.[4] At the same time, the entire episode of the Phaeacians replays on one level Hermes' mission to Ogygia, as a masculine figure infiltrates a feminine milieu, bringing about the release of Odysseus.[5] In this sense it is significant that Odysseus is only named after he has won the Phaeacians over and been given assurances that they will take him home. In both cases, Odysseus is released from a potentially annihilating stasis, reentering time; in both cases, he brings pain to a woman by refusing to relinquish his *nostos* and stay with her.

Odysseus also delivers death to the Phaeacians.[6] The sailors who take him back to Ithaka are presumably turned to stone along with their ship in the harbor at Scheria, a grim reminder of Poseidon's power. Again we hear echoes of the Calypso episode, which ends with Poseidon destroying a ship that has carried Odysseus toward home. Here, of course, others pay for Odysseus' acts, also a common pattern in the poem. Alcinous, seeing the petrified ship, recalls a prophecy from his father that Poseidon would one day punish the Phaeacians for being "kindly escorts" for all travelers who come to them (13.174). The word translated "kindly" here is *apêmones,* literally "without suffering," suggesting that the specific offense of escorting strangers stands here for the society's general tendency to avoid suffering in various forms, through war, conflict with other peoples, the ordinary by-products of regular human interaction.

The second part of the punishment, sealing the Phaeacians off permanently by putting a mountain in their harbor (13.177), further clarifies the effect of Odysseus' visit to Scheria. Now the separation from other societies, which has been a matter of choice and presumably revocable through seafaring, would—if the threat is carried out, and the poem does not tell us if it is—become final.[7] As has often been noted, the Phaeacians are a way station for the hero, an in-between place. Odysseus enters a society that exists in a fantastic middle zone between Calypso's timeless cosmos and the ordinary human world of Ithaka.[8] Because of him, that status may change: the life on Scheria may become "real" in that its inhabitants must hereafter suffer the physical consequences of their separation from others. The blissful Shangri-la may become an isolated island.

In the course of his adventures, Odysseus is continually threatened with death in one form or another, physical destruction from the Laestrygonians, the Cyclops, Scylla and Charybdis, psychic annihilation from the Lotus Eaters, Circe, the Sirens. And men do die but not Odysseus. He pushes on for home, leaving a trail of bodies across the Mediterranean. He begins straightforwardly with the Cicones, killing their men, enslaving their women. But then his crewmen begin to exhibit the lack of self-control that characterizes their collectively inferior character. They refuse to leave before reinforcements arrive from the

Cicones, and six men from each ship are killed (9.43–61). Here begins a string of lethal encounters until Odysseus washes ashore on Calypso's island alone. The degree of his own responsibility for these deaths varies from case to case: he insists that they investigate the Cyclopes' island when there is no practical reason to do so; the same curiosity prompts the visit to Circe, which imperils half the crew; he does not trust the crew enough to tell them why they ought not look in the bag of winds. However we may characterize Odysseus' intentions and their results, the brute fact of mortality follows wherever he goes.

Each of the longer episodes in the adventures, the Cyclops, Circe, Hades, and—as a shorter coda—the Cattle of the Sun, reflects in different ways a complex interaction between anonymity and mortality. In each, the poet draws on older mythic and/or folktale story patterns to explore the effects of Odysseus' arrival in an exotic and threatening venue. A closer look at these episodes will enrich our understanding of the hero and his contradictory character.

POLYPHEMUS

The escape from the Cyclops' cave is the most famous of all Odysseus' adventures. The poet here combines elements from several common folktales into a complex episode that dramatizes central aspects of Odysseus' character and mission.[9] We may begin by noting a common mythic pattern that the episode reflects, the hero's conquest of a chaos monster. In his capacity as defender—or restorer—of order, the ancient hero often finds himself confronted by a creature whose function is to deny in some way the right order of things. To preserve or establish civilization, the hero must subdue this monster and avert chaos. Here we see the "culture hero" who stands in for all of us as we attempt to find meaning by imposing patterns on the seemingly amorphous flux of experience. The pattern is old and ubiquitous in Mediterranean myths: Gilgamesh and the monster of the Cedar forest, Marduk and Tiamat, Apollo and Pytho. Given the clear links between Odysseus' *nostos* and the restoration of order, we can see him in the role of culture hero when he conquers the Cyclops.

Homer's portrait of Polyphemus is not, however, confined to his role as a chaos monster. He does live a brutish existence—expressed most vividly by his cannibalism—and one poorly adapted to the natural features of his island. Though crops grow by themselves in all the fields, he chooses to be a dairy farmer; though the neighboring island features goats, which he keeps along with sheep, neither he nor any of his fellow Cyclopes has ever gone sailing. The Cyclopes and the Phaeacians occupy different ends of the continuum of civilization, but both forgo the benefits of interaction with other cultures. Yet if his way of living is out of tune with his surroundings, Polyphemus does in fact impose a fastidious order on his daily existence.[10] The poet takes pains to describe the monster's minicosmos: sheep and goats carefully divided into groups, newborns in this pen, yearlings in that; cheeses stored on racks, pails and buckets lined up. His routine, too, is unyieldingly regular, moving the herds in and out every day, milking. Like Calypso, the Cyclops presides over an ordered world but not one reflecting a typically human order. Though Odysseus may in one sense be the guardian of *human* order, at the same time he brings chaos to the tidy existence of the monster.

There is, to be sure, something perverse, almost unnatural, in the Cyclops' willful indifference to larger, seemingly more important potential congruities between his surroundings and his way of life. And yet by describing the monster's homely routines the poet also invites a fleeting twinge of sympathy from us. Polyphemus is, by human standards, a murderous lout, but because he lives against the grain (as it were) of his surroundings, his husbandry has a certain fussiness that pulls us toward him, not away. Though huge and ugly, he is also, in his preoccupations, a *small* creature, almost quaint.[11]

The seed thus planted comes into bloom after Odysseus and his men have blinded Polyphemus. The rest of the crew has escaped on the undersides of sheep. Only Odysseus remains inside, clinging to the big ram that rules the flock. Polyphemus has been feeling the backs of the sheep as they exit, and now he puts his hands on the ram, sensing something amiss (9.447–57):

> My dear ram, why have you run out of the cave last
> of all the flock? Never before would you be left behind;
> no, first of all the flock you'd tread the tender new grass
> with big strides; you'd come first to the rushing streams,
> eager to lead the way back to the stalls in the evening.
> Now you're last of all to leave. Are you grieving for the eye
> of your master, the eye that evil man destroyed

with his sorry companions? He clouded my wits with wine,
that Nobody, who I say will never escape destruction!
If only you thought like me, spoke like me, and could tell
me where that man runs from my rage.

The effect of these words is unexpectedly poignant. Polyphemus, alone as always, blind now and presumably helpless, seeks solace from an animal who cannot answer him. The ram becomes in this moment more pet than livestock, responding in his unusual reticence to Polyphemus' wound and its consequences, patiently waiting while his master pours out his pain. The tenderness of the Cyclops here contrasts with his savage behavior toward Odysseus and the crew, emphasizing his vulnerable state.

To this wounded creature the poet contrasts Odysseus, triumphant. He has conquered the monster and paid him back for eating his companions. We should be happy that the hero has escaped with at least some of his crew, that the *nostos* can continue. Yet, as in the Calypso episode, so here the poet creates an adversary who is unexpectedly sympathetic. There is no question of our disapproving of what Odysseus has done to the Cyclops any more than we would hope that Calypso could keep her mortal captive. Polyphemus did, after all, relish eating the crew. But part of what makes the *Odyssey* hold us is the richness with which it presents human action and motivation. Even in the unlikely case of the Cyclops, the poet makes room for second thoughts. Athena leads the cheers for Odysseus, Sacker of Cities, but we may hear echoes of another way to evaluate the consequences of his victory.

As in most of Odysseus' adventures, gender plays a role in the articulation of this episode. As has often been noted, the imagery of birth suffuses the encounter: Odysseus and his men are trapped in a womblike cave, the hero is notoriously nameless until he drives a pointed stake into the round orifice on the monster's face, the pains of the Cyclops are described using the word for birth pains in Greek, and Odysseus reemerges from anonymity in the cave to reclaim his heroic identity.[12] Polyphemus' symbolically female role in the transaction is perhaps paralleled by his housekeeping. The Cyclops episode is the first (in the story's chronology) and most overt example of Odysseus penetrating a feminine milieu and effecting his own rebirth.

Finally, we note that, as he did with the Phaeacians, so here Odysseus effects permanent change in the life of the Cyclops. Before the Greeks arrive, Polyphemus' way of living, though narrow and out of tune with his surroundings, works well enough to support his monocular existence. His rudimentary self-sufficiency ensures that he need not be part of any larger community of Cyclopes, which is just as well since no such community apparently exists. Once blinded, Polyphemus needs his fellow monsters to survive, but because of Odysseus' famous name trick, the others do not respond to his distress. He is, like the Phaeacians, permanently isolated. In this context, the cost of Odysseus' rebirth appears yet more vividly if we revisit the poet's tableau of the Cyclops and his ram. The bloody socket in the monster's forehead replicates in micro the dark opening of the cave out of which Odysseus is about to emerge.

Odysseus again forges ahead, driving onward toward Ithaka. He leaves behind him pain in various forms and also a changed world. I have said that we could see Odysseus, true to his role as the stranger who brings disorder, as the principal agent of mortality and change in the poem. His effect on both the Phaeacians and Polyphemus reflects this role. In a tragic story, the narrative has as its goal the acceptance of limits on human action, with death as the ultimate limit. Though the *Odyssey* as a whole is a comic narrative, driven by the need for restoration of the status quo and thus militating against change, Odysseus' effect on at least some of the places he passes through is to enforce limit, to make final what is only potential. He must return to Ithaka in order to restore order and block change, but along the way he often does just the opposite, creating disorder, enforcing change.

CIRCE

Odysseus comes to Circe first in the story's chronology, but we inevitably see her through Calypso. The two figures are much alike, at least on the surface: minor goddesses who live alone, control their surroundings through spellbinding song, weave, and threaten Odysseus with oblivion. The power of both is represented primarily through sexuality, though Circe is the more transparently allegorical character of the two. When the advance party approaches her house, wolves and lions, tamed by magic drugs, fawn on them. They hear the witch inside her house, "singing with a lovely voice, working at the great immortal loom to make graceful, filmy, shimmering garments such as come from goddesses"

(10.221–23). The men are enthralled, and their leader, Polites, urges them all to call her. She quickly comes out, "opening the shining doors," and welcomes them in. They sit and accept honeyed wine laced with magic drugs, are transformed by a touch of her wand into pigs, and are driven into the sty (10.230–43).

Comparing this passage to Hermes' arrival at Calypso's cave is instructive.[13] In each case, the goddess is out of sight, weaving, but touches the visitor(s) aurally through her enchanting voice, which wafts out of the dwelling; in each case the power of the voice seems to resonate in a mysterious control over natural forces, Calypso's lush "garden," Circe's animals. Because we have already seen Calypso, these parallels might well alert us that a seductive and potentially dangerous creature lives in Circe's house. But the differences between the two passages are even more telling. While Calypso's power creates a beautiful and harmonious natural habitat, orderly but not in the way of human civilization, Circe's magic subdues the two wild animals most often associated through similes in Homeric epic with the raw masculine force of human warriors. Hermes simply enters the cave to find Calypso at her loom, whereas Circe "opens the shining doors," an invitation with clear sexual overtones.[14] Calypso graciously supplies nectar and ambrosia to her fellow god, then inquires politely as to his purpose, following the prescribed etiquette for welcoming guests: refreshment first, questions later. Circe, too, offers a seat and a drink, but the nourishment carries her power in it, making the visitors forget the desire for home, erasing their identities. Although Calypso has been keeping Odysseus from returning home, she has not used her power to make him forget Ithaka and his family. We might even see a reference in the Circe episode to the widespread belief in Mediterranean myth that if one eats with the dead he is doomed to remain with them forever. And finally, of course, the subsequent porcine existence of the crew is a transparently allegorical reference to what sex can bring out in a man.

By having Odysseus send an advance party, the poet allows him (and us) to anticipate the threat Circe poses. The hero apparently has, in fact, no particular plan when he sets out, and Hermes happens across his path as he approaches the witch's lair (10.274–79). Once again the messenger god intervenes on the hero's behalf, though this time we are not told why he appears or who sent him—since we are seeing the events through Odysseus' eyes, the omniscient third-person narrator is not appropriate here.[15] Much has been made of the magic drug, moly, which the god gives to Odysseus to neutralize Circe's power; we should note, however, that once protected he must do his part to subdue the witch (10.293–301):

Whenever Circe touches you with her long wand,
then draw your sharp sword from beside your thigh
and make a thrust as if trying to kill her.
She'll be afraid and urge you to go to bed with her.
Then do not refuse the bed of the goddess,
so she might release your comrades and care for you;
rather demand that she swear a great oath by the immortals
neither to plot any other evil pain for you
once you're naked, nor take away your manhood.

Another mythic paradigm surfaces here, that of the danger a mortal man risks in sleeping with a goddess: death or emasculation.[16] The entire transaction is, in fact, straightforwardly about power expressed through sex. The moly protects Odysseus from the influence of Circe's potions, but he must then subdue her sexually. She invites him in, gives him a seat, and offers a drink. In early Greek epic, to accept both would ordinarily be to acquiesce in some way to the person offering.[17] So here Circe tries to transform Odysseus into a pig, to exert the sexual dominance her potion effects. He pulls out his sword, and she immediately assumes the suppliant position, guessing that he is Odysseus, about whom she has been warned by Hermes, and invites him to bed; he refuses until she swears an oath—Helen surfaces again—not to harm him when he is naked and render him *anênora*, "unmanly" (10.320–44).

The carefully orchestrated entry of Odysseus into Circe's world reminds us again of Calypso but with the events in a different order. On Ogygia, Odysseus is becalmed first and subject to the nymph's sexual power, then Hermes releases him, then he himself guarantees his final immunity from her influence—expressed by the cloak that is dragging him under water—by getting Ino's veil, a symbolic surrender by the nymph of her modesty, which counterbalances Calypso's lingering hold on him. Here the magic talisman comes first, then the sexual power negotiation, which leaves Odysseus in possession of his manliness, then sex with him in the dominant role. The danger of being trapped in a timeless feminized oblivion—less starkly put here since the Calypso episode has already dramatically established Odysseus' attitude toward such a fate—is eliminated by a preemptive masculine strike. He does linger for a year with the goddess, and must be recalled to his duty, but there is no hint of coercion. Indeed, once the power struggle is over, Circe becomes entirely benign, never refusing Odysseus the help he needs to sail on toward Ithaka.[18]

The dynamic of the entire Circe episode is, then, different from Odysseus' encounters with Calypso, the Phaeacians, or Polyphemus. In each of these earlier episodes, Odysseus enters a society in which the way of life presents an existential threat to him. In each case he surmounts the danger, is symbolically reborn, and leaves behind him a residue of pain. His advent brings some kind of permanent change in each place, making concrete what was implicit. This is true even of Calypso's existence, because the poet has taken care to make her attachment to Odysseus genuine and believable, so that his leaving causes her pain, even though she is a goddess. None of this happens in the Circe episode, which exists in the narrative as a basically comic interlude in which there are no permanent consequences for the inhabitants of her island and none for Odysseus' crew except for Elpenor's death, about which they only learn after leaving Aeae and going to the underworld. The event with the greatest mythic charge, the changing of men into pigs, is, like Odysseus' disguises, reversible.

If Circe is more transparently allegorical than Calypso, she is also less engaging as a personality. Unlike Calypso, she has no significant emotional connection to Odysseus, nor he to her—beyond gratitude for her help—and his leaving arouses no strong emotions in either of them or in us. In this sense, the witch stands in for Athena, a powerful goddess who can help the hero but asks little in return. Indeed, the episode offers a microcosmic view of the centripetal *nostos* plot. First, the hero must assert himself in a way that brings recognition of his *kleos* and puts him in control of the situation in general and a woman in particular; then he lives at his ease with a beautiful woman who provides him with the comforts of home. Penelope is, of course, far from a two-dimensional character, and winning her over takes more than the brandishing of a sword. We also know that Odysseus does have a profound attachment to his wife since he has chosen her over an immortal nymph.

Yet precisely because we know of his great love for Penelope, we may experience some difficulty understanding why the crew must come to Odysseus, after a year on Aeae, to ask him to leave Circe. There is no ducking this question: the poet did not need to tell the story in such a way as to point insistently at Odysseus's decision to linger. We can simply conclude that Circe's attractions are obvious and that a double standard in regard to marital fidelity is commonplace in early Greek literature. But viewed alongside Odysseus' reunion with Penelope the episode puts the focus squarely on the tensions we encounter in the plot of the poem and the character of Odysseus.

The parallels between Circe and Penelope are intriguing. Both are weavers; both are subject to divine influence that makes them easier for Odysseus to win over; once the testing of the hero, which results in the reaffirmation of his identity, is past, both companions are loving, completely supportive, and—once subdued—not vividly interesting. Like Odysseus, Penelope engages us most when asserting herself and—in her own way—winning *kleos*. Confronted with an anonymous stranger, both Circe and Penelope show power and resourcefulness; once Odysseus has been revealed, they exude much less electricity. We will never know exactly why Homer chose to emphasize Odysseus' puzzling reluctance to leave Circe. Perhaps the episode confirms retrospectively—from our point of view as external audience—the threat that Odysseus faces on Calypso's island: he learns from his sojourn what his true priorities are. In any event, though his dallying is out of tune with the imperatives of the *nostos* plot, the episode taken as a whole mirrors that plot and offers insights into the elements of the story that undermine it.

HADES

Like the Polyphemus episode, the trip to the underworld in book 11 initially invokes a powerful mythic paradigm. The *katabasis* is the oldest and most profound of all the archetypal adventures associated in ancient literature and myth with the hero's journey. Traveling to the land of the dead brings the hero face-to-face with mortality, the defining element of human existence; to make the journey and return to tell of it is to transcend ordinary boundaries of experience, to be reborn knowing what cannot be known by ordinary people. The darkness of the land of the dead can also become a metaphor for the inner recesses of the human psyche, a fertile terrain for pursuing self-knowledge.[19]

The *katabasis* is most often found in tragic narratives, where the hero, in order to reach a full understanding of his nature, must accept the fact of his own mortality. Gilgamesh's journey to the Land of Dilmun is the earliest example we know. Frightened by the death of his friend Enkidu, Gilgamesh travels across the waters of darkness to question Utnapishtim, the only mortal to achieve immortality, about "the secret of life and death." The hero wants to escape death, but Utnapishtim tells him that no one else may do so, and Gilgamesh returns to Uruk to rule as king and live within the limits placed on all mortals. The motif appears in a different form in the *Iliad,* where the hell that Achilles visits is his own inner darkness, variously represented in the story, and his acceptance is signaled by the two long speeches he makes to Priam in book 24.[20]

We would not expect the *Odyssey,* as a comic narrative in which the goal of the story is to resist change, with a hero who is steadfastly closed off from influence by others, to draw on the trip to the underworld as a venue for transformation. Circe sends Odysseus to Hades to find out from Tiresias how to get home, but in fact he learns something quite different from the old prophet: how he will die. In this sense, Odysseus does confront the fact of his mortality and quite directly. Tiresias instructs him to travel inland until he finds a society with no knowledge of the sea, to sacrifice to Poseidon, and then to return home to await a "gentle death," which will come from the sea in his old age (11.119–37). The details are tantalizing: Odysseus must escape the sea, a symbol elsewhere in the poem of disorder and oblivion, and then make peace with Poseidon, his chief tormentor and the god most intent on erasing him from the earth; if he follows the prophet's instructions, the death that eventually takes him will be "gentle," not violent, and only when he is old.

Yet if the sea is the venue for Odysseus' persecution by external forces, it is also—true to the tensions within the hero—a symbol of the restless motion that characterizes his quest for *kleos.* To find rest, he must propitiate both the inner and the outer obstacles to his *nostos.* We remember that Odysseus reveals the prophecy to Penelope while the two are having a postcoital chat in book 23. Finally at rest with his wife, he tells her what he says will please neither her nor him, that he must go roving again (23.265–84). In his retelling, Odysseus repeats the prophecy, in typical Homeric fashion, nearly verbatim: he will be doing some traveling in the near future, raiding for spoils (23.357) and also settling up with Poseidon. The centrifugal Odysseus is speaking here, reasserting himself, however gently, in the presence of his wife, who represents one important part of the overall goal of the centripetal *nostos* plot.

Homer does not tell us anything about Tiresias beyond the fact that he is a blind prophet. Nothing in the narrative alludes to the stories we encounter about him in later literature, his role in the Oedipus plays of Sophocles or in the curious story that makes Tiresias the only human to have lived as both a man and a woman.[21] If we do assume those stories as background for the episode in *Odyssey* 11, they suggest for the old man a certain gender ambiguity. In *Oedipus Tyrannos* and *Oedipus at Colonus*, Tiresias represents a foil for Oedipus' more typically masculine persona: blind and thus unable to assert himself in the world in the way of masculine heroes but blessed with inner wisdom to compensate, a passive conduit for Apollo's wisdom and power rather than an active agent.[22] In Ovid's vignette, which happens to be the first full accounting of the myth of a transgendered prophet but may well reflect a much older story, Tiresias is walking in the woods and comes across two snakes copulating. He hits them with a stick and is transformed into a woman. Seven years later, she is walking in the woods again, sees two snakes copulating, hits them, and is changed back into a man. He now has experience that makes him the best human to resolve the dispute between Juno and Jupiter about which sex has the most pleasure during intercourse. He says that women have more pleasure, and Juno strikes him blind; Jupiter gives him the art of prophecy as compensation.

We can never know what other stories might have been assumed to be attached to Tiresias. But in any event, as Bassi has recently argued, the land of the dead as it appears in the *Odyssey* is in many other ways a feminized milieu, a "land of women," as she puts it.[23] Much of Odysseus' time is spent viewing the parade of women, and the male heroes he sees are, like all *psychai*, strengthless wraiths who can only be energized briefly by drinking blood. The dominant theme of his exchanges with dead heroes is their yearning for life—any kind of life—rather than the impotence they experience in Hades. They ask about their fathers and sons, who might perpetuate their name in the world above, never about their mothers or daughters. Achilles is the vehicle for the most vivid of these speeches. Odysseus hails him as being powerful over the dead, as he was over the living, but Achilles will have none of it: he would rather be alive as a slave to a nobody than a king in Hades; he asks for news of his son and father, thirsting for life in any form, wishing he could be alive to protect his father, to wreak havoc on the old man's enemies in his father's house, *pateros dô* (11.488–503). No dead hero can win *kleos* through action.

For Odysseus, of course, Hades also is the home of his mother, as opposed to Ithaka, which is still the house of his father. Her very name aligns Odysseus' mother with all that would negate his existence: Antikleia, "against glory." His questions of her place him for the moment on a level with the heroes who have already died: what of his father, his son, his wife? It is as if by coming into contact with his mother Odysseus experiences *antikleia* in the strengthless oblivion of death. He also asks her how she came to Hades and learns that she died of longing for him, for his counsel and sweetness. Antikleia here stands in for Penelope, who awaits the return of her husband, and also presents, in her desire to keep Odysseus home, an obstacle to the winning of *kleos*. At the same time, the reference to Epikaste—Homer's name for the mother of Oedipus—in the catalog of women suggests another danger for Odysseus in Hades, another threat to his heroic *kleos*. In a broader sense, as Bassi points out, the "house of Hades" (10.491, 512) is a domestic space ordinarily associated with women in Greek epic.[24] The fates of both Agamemnon and Oedipus illustrate the dangers of returning to a space controlled by women: the father's house may turn out to be a mother's house.

Odysseus' *katabasis* replays, then, the familiar pattern: masculine penetration of a feminized milieu, resulting in the rebirth of Odysseus. We might suppose that, since the dead are presumably beyond the troubles of this world, Odysseus would not be able to cause pain in Hades as he does elsewhere. But the blood in the ditch enlivens the ghosts, making them vulnerable to the hero who brings trouble with him wherever he goes: Agamemnon, Achilles, Ajax, Antikleia, all express pain that Odysseus has reanimated along with the dead souls. The *katabasis* demonstrates a hero's extraordinary powers, his ability to transcend mortality. In this case, the hero brings the dead back to life—or far enough back to feel pain.

Although he affects others, this rebirth, like all the others he experiences along the way to Ithaka, does not seem to result in an inner transformation in Odysseus. His experiences in Hades would certainly lead us to expect some change as a result of his journey into darkness. He has spoken to figures from his past, who represent attitudes and ways of being with powerful implications for him. Agamemnon, Achilles, Herakles, and Ajax, each in his own way, reflect back to him heroic characteristics from the perspective of the dead. The catalogs of women show him victims of the kind of masculine assertion he has practiced so often on his journey, and Antikleia mirrors issues central to his identity as a man, a son, and a husband. Finally, from Tiresias Odysseus learns something about the nature of his own death, a wisdom ordinarily denied mortals. Yet, although his resolve to punish the suitors may be reinforced by his exchanges with Agamemnon, Achilles, and Antikleia, we see nothing in Odysseus analogous to the shifts of perspective in either Gilgamesh or Achilles as a result of these encounters.

We are not surprised, as I have said, to see the hero resist transformation. But in any event, he has been shielded in advance from any vulnerability. Here, as in the Circe episode, he protects himself with his drawn sword, controlling access to liveliness in the ghosts. And once again we see the *nostos* plot reflected obliquely. His arrival in the underworld can effect no permanent change, as is the case on the island of Circe. Both places mirror, in this sense, the Ithaka that Odysseus must restore to fulfill the *nostos* plot; in both places—and, presumably, in the restored Ithaka—no *kleos,* and thus no heroic identity, can be created. From this perspective all three venues represent the stasis that is equated so often in the poem with death.

THE CATTLE OF THE SUN

At first glance, the story of the Cattle of the Sun does not fit easily into the series of episodes we have been pursuing in this chapter. There is no society for Odysseus to encounter, no detaining woman. He is warned twice not to visit Thrinacia and tries to heed the advice. As in the Aeolus episode, his companions disobey his warnings, showing the lack of self-control that characterizes their behavior generally, and pay with their lives: when Odysseus finally arrives on the island of Calypso, he is alone. Yet because of its position at the end of the adventures, certain elements in the episode are charged with meaning.

We are perhaps not surprised to find that the guardians of the flocks for Helios are female, the nymphs Phaëthousa and Lampetiê. The cattle themselves are *kalai boes* (12.262), the feminine form of the adjective in Greek suggesting that these are cows not bulls. In other words, it is a feminine milieu. This is tantalizing given the gendered nature of the other episodes we have been describing. Although it is something of a stretch to see the cattle as animal versions of Circe, the gendered aspects of the episode combined with the connection of the herds with the phenomenon of time does bring the episode into line with those preceding it.

There are, we are told, 350 head of cattle and 350 sheep, numbers never changed by birth or death. Thinkers as early as Aristotle have seen the number of animals as reflecting the days in the year, a reasonable conclusion given that they belong to the sun. Austin has suggested that to kill the cattle is to attack time itself, surely a grave offense.[25] But given that the adventure concludes a string of episodes that exemplify the tension between centripetal and centrifugal forces, between *kleos* and *nostos,* it is the static existence of the herds that captures our attention.

The Greeks are told not to kill any of the animals or, to put it another way, not to bring death into the perfect, unchanging world of Thrinacia. To do so will imperil the *nostos.* Immediately before Odysseus finally arrives back on Ithaka, where the tensions of the narrative will come to a crescendo, the poet tells a story that exemplifies those tensions in a symbolic form: to restore the world as it should be, Odysseus must return home and reverse the changes that time has brought to Ithaka; the cattle of the sun embody that imperative. The Odysseus who tries to restrain his companions is entirely centripetal, not the curious explorer of the Polyphemus and Circe episodes. His behavior here, just before he begins his vengeance on the suitors, is perhaps the best argument for the idea that he has learned from his mistakes, has seen the dangers of willful self-assertion. Whether that learning reflects a significant change in perspective or a perfecting of skills already present is another question.

CONCLUSION: THE STRANGER WHO IS NOT A STRANGER

In the longer episodes of books 9–12, Odysseus plays out the implications of the motif of the arrival of the stranger in various ways. He invariably brings disorder and pain; he sometimes effects significant change; he himself, by contrast, does not change. When he is named, he becomes the "stranger who is not a stranger," and the transition from anonymity to celebrity offers us further insights into the issues of identity central to the poem's meaning. To explore them fully, we must look beyond the official stance of the *Odyssey,* that anonymity is a form of death, that in order to be, the hero must be known.

When Odysseus arrives at a new place along the way home, we have seen that his appearance as a stranger is often characterized as a kind of rebirth, after which he progresses toward his full powers, which are certified by his being named. In this sense—as has often been noted—each of the larger episodes in books 5 through 12 is a rehearsal for Odysseus' full return to himself in book 23. We have also seen that the poem reflects a continuing tension between the *nostos* plot, which has rest in Ithaka as its goal, and the restless self-assertion that fuels Odysseus' quest for *kleos*. Odysseus can only be fully himself, we are told, when he reassumes the roles of king, husband, father, and son. At the same time, the implied parallels between Hades and Ithaka, between Penelope and the various "detaining women" of the story, hint that to rest in Ithaka is in some sense to die.

Odysseus' alternation between the poles of celebrity and anonymity articulates his progress through the poem. The relationship of this polarity to that between *nostos* and *kleos* adds further complexity to the narrative. Athena works for Odysseus' return to his full powers, as they are displayed in his position on Ithaka. For her, as for the striving hero, namelessness is finally to be avoided. And yet, by controlling access to his identity Odysseus gains some leverage when entering a new society: to be nobody can have its advantages. The most obvious example of this is the Cyclops episode, which makes the flexibility of namelessness a central theme in the episode. Odysseus gets the better of the monster because he is not known. Being Odysseus in that instance would have put the Cyclops on guard and obviated his punning stratagems. Perhaps the same might be said of the Circe episode, where Odysseus' anonymity helps him take the witch by surprise.

Again the return plot points us toward a particular set of assumptions: nothing is more important than for Odysseus to return home and vanquish the suitors; to do so he will need extraordinary power; since knowledge brings power in the *Odyssey*, controlling others' access to knowledge about him will always benefit Odysseus. But this calculus, driven by a narrowly defined set of goals, excludes modes of experiencing life that do not fit its objectives. If we step away from these imperatives, a different picture emerges. Anonymity, for example, can make entrance into and movement within a new place easier. While one's identity might open doors, it could close them just as well. The change that comes over Achilles in book 24 of the *Iliad* is instructive in this regard. His speech to

Priam urges the old man toward acceptance of Hector's mortality, the one thing, above all others, that defines humans as opposed to gods. All of human life can be understood as a series of gifts from the gods, some helpful, some harmful, none to be refused (*Iliad* 24.518–51). The perspective that Achilles urges on the old man sees all humans as if from above, indistinguishable from that great height, joined in their limitations. To see in this way is a radical departure for the hero, who customarily measures himself against all other mortals: is he the tallest, the swiftest, the strongest? And what certifies his stature is, of course, *kleos*. *Kleos* separates, anonymity unites.

The stranger can also blend quickly with a group in part because, as we have said, the group is eager to bring him in and confer some kind of identity on him as a means of control: because it brings disorder and change, the unknown can be dangerous, as many of Odysseus' hosts discover. Firm identity, by contrast, assigns status and places boundaries around the persona: a handsome stranger can marry Nausicaa and prosper in a land of aesthetic refinement; Odysseus cannot. Order is prerequisite to memory, memory to *kleos,* and *kleos* to the fixed identity that must endure if Athena's plans are to be realized. All of this brings us back to the tension between open and closed worlds. The secret, which Athena does not want us to discover, is that namelessness and its attendant disorder are also creative, opening up new worlds. Change can come from chance when the boundaries of the known are breached and fortuity leaks through. We turn again to Kermode:

> One bolder view would be that an ideal text would be perfectly fortuitous, that only the fractures are of interest; that in establishing coherence we reduce the text to codes implanted in our minds by the arbitrary fiat of a culture or an institution, and are therefore the unconscious victims of ideological oppression. Freedom, the freedom to produce meaning, rests in fortuity, the removal of constraints on sense.[26]

As he draws closer to the triumphant act of violence that seals his *nostos,* Odysseus, paradoxically it would seem, becomes more creative in his namelessness.

Chapter Four

CONSTRUCTED LIVES

For what is "identity" but our power to control others' definitions of us?

Joyce Carol Oates

Book 13 marks the return of Odysseus to Ithaka and the return of Athena to the story. As she becomes more visible, the goals of the return plot come to the fore. From now on, we will be reminded frequently of the nefarious suitors, gluttonously devouring Odysseus' goods, of Penelope's struggle to hold out against their importunities. As Odysseus schemes in book 13 with his divine protector and then in book 16 with his son, we experience all the vicarious pleasures that accompany the revenge plot, cheering for the hero, watching his benighted enemies as they march unknowingly to their doom. Secrecy, disguise, lying, manipulation of the innocent and the evil, all are welcome to us if we give ourselves over to the imperatives of the restoration. Because we are impatient for the action to begin, the interlude at Eumaeus' outpost can seem tedious, uneventful.[1]

But there are other pleasures available to us in books 13–16 and other ways to understand what is at stake when Odysseus finally returns. The key to this alternative perspective is in the many biographies and autobiographies, true and false, that we hear in this part of the poem. Relationships develop before us between Athena and Odysseus, Eumaeus

65

and the old stranger, Telemachus and Theoclymenus, Telemachus and Odysseus. Nearly everyone in this section of the poem is initially a stranger to those he meets and comes into being, for them and us, through the stories he tells. Whereas the return plot depends on a model of the self as fixed and unchanging, the personae we encounter in the countryside are created relationally through narratives. In this milieu, we see most clearly the poem's alternate vision of human life as uncertain, difficult, limited by time, chance, and the ordinary frailties that beset us all. The people we meet here—as opposed to the invincible hero sheltered by a goddess—need each other to survive. Odysseus' drive toward continuing self-definition is part of this other world, and as he draws ever closer to the triumphant affirmation of his unchanging status in Ithaka, his urge to create himself anew becomes—as if in response—yet more assertive.[2]

ITHAKA REVISITED

When the Phaeacians leave the sleeping Odysseus on the shores of his homeland, we, along with the hero, return to much that is by now familiar. Odysseus is symbolically reborn yet again: he falls into a deep sleep, "like death," on the Phaeacians' boat (13.80); he awakens to a seemingly new world, full of anxiety about who lives there:

> Oh no, what sort of people are these, whose land I've reached?
> Are they arrogant, fierce, and lacking in justice?
> Or kind to strangers, with intelligence like the gods'?

These lines repeat verbatim his exclamation when he awakens on Scheria, with the voices of Nausicaa and her friends wafting around his head (13.200–202 = 6.119–21). He is, as far as he can tell, once again a stranger in a strange land. He meets a young man, apparently noble, just as he meets a well-mannered young woman on the beach at Scheria. This time, however, it is Athena in disguise. In response to his questions, the young man exclaims that he must be a fool if he has not heard of Ithaka (13.237–49). "Why yes," he replies, "I seem to remember hearing something about it when I was in Crete . . ."[3]

So begins the first of Odysseus' "false tales." He is from Crete (famous in antiquity as the nurse of liars);[4] he is on the run now, having murdered a fellow countryman under whose father he refused to serve at Troy, preferring to captain his own troop; he is in Ithaka by accident, having set out as a passenger on a Phoenician ship headed for Pylos or Elis; and a storm blew them off course and they arrived in Ithaka instead (13.256–86). The story has many features that will be become familiar in the next few books: a traveler from Crete, the Phoenicians providing transport, a fugitive murderer. Indeed, some of this history also recalls stories about Patroclus and Phoenix in the *Iliad* (*Iliad* 9.444–79; 23.83–92). Odysseus is predictably cautious with this stranger, withholding his real identity until he knows the young man better. His choice of lies is in some ways understandable: Crete is far enough away to make it unlikely that any local person would know enough to refute his story, and the Phoenicians were the premier sailors in antiquity. But why does he claim to be a murderer, even providing details of his sneaky ambush?

First of all, Odysseus does provide an engagingly racy persona—appearing as a elderly farmer who fell asleep on the ship by mistake would simply not make as good a story for the young man or for us. But beyond pure entertainment value, Odysseus' claim to be a murderer might also put the young man on notice that this stranger ought to be handled with care and at a distance. Others may prefer to reach out to a potential host but not Odysseus, who is concerned always to control access to himself.

Athena's reaction to the story is immediate and warm (13.291–300):

So he spoke, and the gray-eyed goddess Athena smiled
and caressed him with her hand. She made herself like a woman,
beautiful and tall and adept at weaving lovely things.
She addressed him and spoke winged words:
"Crafty and sly would be the man who got around you,
with all your tricks, even if a god encountered you.
Tough, wily, never tired of lies, you were not about
to let go of deception—even here in your own land—
and deceitful stories, so dear to you.
But come now, let's not talk anymore of these things;
we both are versed in the arts of cunning, since you are best
of all men at plots and speeches, and I among the gods
am famed for my wits and craft. But even you didn't know
Pallas Athena, daughter of Zeus . . .

Athena's delight at Odysseus does not surprise us at this point, nor does the fact that she loves him because he is like her—Homeric gods admire themselves above all others. Odysseus' reply, acknowledging her past help and pressing her for confirmation that this is really Ithaka, brings another burst of approbation from the goddess and another analysis by her of his heroic character: discreet, self-possessed, prudent (13.330–32). These adjectives have often been cited as definitive for Odysseus' character.[5] We may also note that, once again, they apply equally well to his patroness.

The fact that Odysseus lies to Athena is not—from her perspective—a bad thing because by doing so he behaves as she does, using his wits to control others. And in the perspective of the centripetal *nostos* plot, all stratagems are to be admired if they lead to the proper conclusion. The plotting begins in earnest now, and Athena debases the hero, rendering him old and wrinkled. Once again, he can be the "stranger who is not a stranger." The disguise will be crucial to his success in Ithaka, but it also has its uses beforehand in the visit to Eumaeus' outpost. An old man will not threaten the swineherd, and since he would presumably have seen something of life, his stories will have the air of authenticity. Odysseus' disguise will advance his plans for revenge, pushing him and us always toward the climax in book 22. But the scenes in the countryside also create meaning in the poem's present.

EUMAEUS' WORLD

The sojourn with Eumaeus again offers familiar pleasures. The faithful servant lives a humble but orderly existence, his lodge surrounded by walls of rough-cut stone topped by a fence of wild pear trees. Outside the walls, a further palisade of stakes driven into the ground, inside, twelve sties, with fifty sows in each. The boars—exactly 360 of them (some cosmological significance here?)—are kept apart from their prospective mates. Later we learn that Eumaeus also has charge of Odysseus' livestock on the mainland, twelve herds each of cattle, sheep, goats, and pigs. He is not alone but himself commands four servants, and each day one of them takes one animal to the suitors. When he enters the outpost, Odysseus encounters a minicosmos, as he did on Ogygia and the island of the Cyclops.[6]

He is greeted rudely at the gate by four snarling dogs, throws aside his staff, and prudently sits down. His mortification continues: the staff, though here the prop of a beggar, can also be the sign of the leader who convenes the assembly. By throwing it down, Odysseus echoes the gesture both of Achilles in *Iliad* 1, when he relinquishes his role as a leader among the Greek forces (1.245), and of Telemachus, who storms petulantly in the assembly of locals he has convened on Ithaka (*Odyssey* 2.80). By making himself so lowly, Odysseus of course prepares the way for his infiltration of the palace. But then again, being a nameless mendicant will also remove barriers that would exist between the king and his servant, however loyal.

The presence of animals at the entrance echoes the birds on Calypso's island, Circe's wolves, the artificial dogs at the entrance of Alcinous' palace. The poet likes to provide a carefully calibrated foil for the human (or divine) intelligence that informs each settlement. The humble hound Argos will later perform the same function at the palace of Odysseus, however briefly. Here the ferocity of the dogs reminds us how precariously Eumaeus holds chaos at bay in the countryside and, by extension perhaps, how close it is to the palace. At the same time, we wonder whether Odysseus will effect the same kind of change in the enclosed world of Eumaeus as he has elsewhere when entering incognito.

Eumaeus rushes to the stranger's aid just in time, driving off the dogs. He is annoyed (14.37–47):

> Old man, a minute more and those dogs would have torn you up,
> and you would have covered me with shame; add this
> to the other pain and trouble the gods have given me!
> Here I sit, aching and groaning for my godlike master,
> fattening up sleek sows for other men to eat,
> while that man wanders the earth looking for food
> in the fields and towns of strangers,
> if he is even still alive and looking at the sun's light.
> But come now, let's go to my hut, old man, so that
> you can satisfy your heart's desire for food and wine
> and then tell me where you're from and what you've suffered.

The disguise is working well: Eumaeus sees only an old beggar, one who will have stories to tell of his hard life. Since he is entertaining someone apparently equal to or even below him on the social scale, the swineherd feels no compunction about inviting the stranger into his hut for a meal.

As the host begins to tell his story, the greedy suitors make their appearance once again as foils for the miserable Odysseus, who Eumaeus is certain will never return to Ithaka. The swineherd circles back to his own despair three more times in the next 150 lines, despite the old man's avowal that the king will indeed return and soon: the suitors have found out somehow that Odysseus is dead, and the gluttons have thrown all restraint to the winds (14.89–95); drifters prey on Penelope's yearning to see her husband again, telling lies to get food, but the bones of Odysseus are bleaching in the sun on some deserted beach (14.122–38); the beggar swears Odysseus will return soon, but no, he's dead, and Telemachus, too, has left home, probably doomed to be murdered by the suitors (14.166–90). This dynamic, of someone who loves Odysseus expressing pessimism about his return in the presence of someone who is at that moment hastening the return, will recur several times in the poem, reaching a crescendo with Penelope's stubborn pessimism in book 23.[7]

The motif's first appearance is in book 1, when Telemachus pours out his anguish to the disguised Athena (1.158–68).

> My dear stranger, would you be offended if I spoke to you?
> Men like those over there care only for flutes and songs;
> life's easy: they eat up the stores of another man,
> whose white bones rot in the rain somewhere,
> lying on a beach, or rolling in the surf.
> If these men were to discover he had come back to Ithaka,
> they'd all pray to be faster on their feet
> rather than richer in gold and fine clothing.
> But now he's suffered an evil fate, and there's no
> comfort left for us, even if someone from somewhere
> should say he's coming home. No, his homecoming's lost.

The echo of Telemachus' pessimism here in Eumaeus' protestations is in fact part of a larger set of parallels between the two scenes. Each is marked strongly by dramatic irony, crucial to the power of the *nostos* plot; each features the motif of the stranger who is not a stranger; and behind each is the old and ubiquitous folktale of the disguised god who enters the home of a powerless, debased person and receives better hospitality there than in the palace of the king.[8] The feeling generated is that the rich and powerful—the suitors in both cases, unworthy surrogates for the proper royal family—will incur the wrath of the god for their bad behavior while the powerless will be rewarded for their selflessness.

There will be another abbreviated replay of the scene in book 16, where Telemachus expresses his despair in the presence of his father (16.192–200). In all three instances, when we are feeling the imperatives of the return, both Telemachus and Eumaeus fuel by their generosity our desire to see the suitors punished for their omissions. We tend not to notice from this perspective that in both cases, as so often in the poem, Odysseus brings pain to those who love him. The desire to see the king again, mixed with certainty that he is dead, creates grief. In this sense, the hero hurts Telemachus, Eumaeus, Penelope, and others in the same way he hurts Antikleia. One might well object that it is hardly his fault that the suitors have moved in and are behaving so badly. And yet the strategy of withholding himself from those who love him, in order to test their loyalty, is not without its costs and might give us pause if we were not convinced that anything Odysseus does that forwards his return is valid regardless of its effect on others.

We may pause to consider the implications of Odysseus playing the role of the disguised god in his encounter with Eumaeus. Insofar as we understand him thus, we see his interactions with the swineherd from a doubled perspective. That is, the emotional authenticity of these exchanges is undermined from the beginning: while he seems to be forming connections with his servant and the latter with him, the entire transaction is based on false assumptions made by Eumaeus, who thinks he is coming to know a needy old man. He experiences the relationship as motivated by the present circumstances of his companion; Odysseus may also be moved in the moment, but he always sees Eumaeus as an instrument to be used for the purpose of achieving his goals. The servant thinks the exchange is one between relative equals; the disguised master operates on the assumption that his priorities, like those of a god among mortals, are paramount.

LIFE STORIES

After supper Eumaeus prevails on his guest to tell his story. Odysseus obliges with his longest and most elaborate yarn. Once again he is from Crete, this time the bastard son of a rich man. When his father died, he was given a paltry inheritance by his half siblings but won a good wife for himself by his own efforts. He was good at battles, ambushes, and face-to-face combat and loved wars and seafaring—nine different raids before the Trojan adventure. Some god put that love in him, but he never liked staying at home farming and raising children: "Different men delight in different things" (14.228). Then he and Idomeneus spent ten years at Troy—each commanding his own troops—and sailed back to Crete. He stayed home only a month, and then his spirit urged him to launch an expedition against Egypt.

It began well but ended in disaster. He intended to scout first, but his crew lost control of themselves and began plundering farms and taking women. The Egyptian armies routed his men, and he escaped death only by throwing himself on the mercy of the king, who spared him. He stayed there for seven years, amassing wealth, and then set sail again, this time with a crafty Phoenician, who promised to take him home with him but in fact planned to sell him into slavery. Zeus cut that plan short with a huge storm, which sank the Phoenician ships and left Odysseus clinging to a lone mast. He washed up on the shores of Thesprotia, there to be saved by the son of Pheidon, the king. He heard there all about Odysseus, who had just left to consult the oracle at Dodona about how to best make his return to Ithaka. The Thesprotians were ready to take the hero back to Ithaka, but before he returned from the oracle Pheidon put him aboard another Thesprotian vessel, supposedly headed for Dulichion and the King Acastus, but—again—there was treachery afoot: once out of harbor, the crew overpowered him with the intention of selling him into slavery. He finally escaped when the ship put in at Ithaka and hid until the Thesprotians gave up looking for him (14.192–359).

Scale marks importance in Homeric poetry, and after the adventures in books 9–12, this is the longest story Odysseus tells. The tale has some affinities to his first effort for Athena: Cretan origins, treacherous enemies, ambush, Phoenician sailors, storms at sea. There are also parallels to the life stories of Eumaeus and Theoclymenus, both yet to come. Eumaeus, too, was the son of a rich man, but he was not so lucky, having been kidnapped by a treacherous Phoenician slave, a woman seduced by sailors from her native land, who then sold the little prince into slavery (15.403–53). Theoclymenus' story—told by the poet not the seer himself—also features trouble over a woman, two murders, and flight (15.222–64).[9]

These stories come from a world far different from the settled life we
have seen in the palaces of the rich. Rootless and restless, moving easily
into and out of various cultures, most of the people we meet in books
13–16 scuffle along on the margins of the great, lying if need be and
looking out for the main chance. Death, in war or by murder, is ever
present, and life is more precarious generally than in Pylos, Sparta, or
Ithaka. These people live every day the existence that the centripetal
Odysseus experiences as temporary on his return journey; change, not
stability, is the dominant feature of their lives. Unlike the Odysseus of the
nostos, whose identity is anchored in a particular place and affirmed by
property, these drifters of necessity create themselves on the fly.[10]

In a world of impermanence, human connection, however random,
however fleeting, can take on great importance. Because no one here is
famous, the separation fostered by *kleos* gives way to relationships easily
formed, as the stories we overhear in this section of the poem create the
basis for connection. And because everyone is a stranger to those he
meets, the stories also offer the context for self-creation: the old beggar
comes into being for Eumaeus entirely through his autobiography. The
urgency that often marks the *nostos* plot recedes for a time as we and the
characters in the story settle back to be entertained by the adventures
that a stranger can provide:

(Odysseus)
Well then, I'll tell you the whole story truthfully.
If the two of us only had the time and enough food
and sweet wine here inside your hut to dine undisturbed
while others busied themselves with work; easily then
I could talk for a whole year and not be done telling
of the pains in my heart, all the many I've suffered
by the gods' will . . . (14.192–98)

(Eumaeus)
Stranger, since you asked me about these things,
sit there quietly and enjoy drinking your wine.
The nights are endless, good for sleeping, good
for enjoying a long story; no need to go to bed
early—too much sleep can be boring. But if
anyone else's heart urges him, let him go to sleep.

And when the dawn comes, he can make a meal
from the master's pigs.
The two of us can eat and drink, taking pleasure
in the memory of each other's sufferings.
Even in the midst of pain a man can enjoy himself,
one who has wandered and suffered much. (15.390–401)

The idea expressed here, that pain encountered after the fact through
the prism of stories can bring a kind of pleasure, is at the heart of the
Odyssey's mediation on the role of art in human life.

Books 13–16 offer an alternative perspective to the heroic vision that
informs so much of Homeric poetry in general and the return plot in
particular. Fame is both the marker of and basis for power in the Homeric poems. Once gained, power must be guarded and, if possible, in-
creased. The hierarchies of status based on power must also be preserved: the suitors are unworthy and must be removed; the loyalty of
both queens and servants is always suspect. To be powerful, then, creates
the need for caution in human relationships and can therefore isolate.
Kleos brings one before the admiring gaze of many but into intimate contact with few. The exchanges in the Ithakan countryside are hampered
by none of these considerations. Strangers with apparently little leverage
in the world can form friendships without worrying about whether their
property will be safe. A rough cloak can be shared without ceremony,
meals without calculation of profit and loss. The principal medium of exchange here is the very experience of pain and trouble: a good story re-
pays the host who feeds the storyteller.[11]

THE LIVES OF ODYSSEUS

While Odysseus himself plays many roles in the course of the poem, others also function as surrogates for him. Telemachus, as has often been
noted, foreshadows many of his father's actions while on his journey to
Pylos and Sparta. Menelaus' story of being trapped in Egypt and then released by a friendly nymph previews Odysseus' captivity on the island of
Calypso and subsequent negotiation with the nymph Leukothea.[12] In
both of these cases, we see a typical Homeric method of characterization
at work. The poet builds meaning by accretion, repeating and elaborat-
ing patterns of action throughout both epics. Thus the portrait of

Diomedes in *Iliad* 5–6 prepares us for Achilles in books 19–22, and Patroclus' foray in Achilles' armor in books 16–17 suggests another paradigm in the making. In the latter case, the poet makes overt reference to the motif by noting that Patroclus puts on all of the armor but cannot wield the Pelian ash spear, which only Achilles can use. A similar moment arrives at the contest of the bow, when Odysseus prevents his son from stringing the bow, his personal emblem of strength.

Telemachus, in fact, begins to function again as a surrogate for Odysseus as soon as he returns to the palace in book 17. There he tells his mother about his adventures, as his father will do later. When descending the stairs to meet her son, Penelope is described as looking "like Artemis or golden Aphrodite" (17.37), a striking simile that only appears once elsewhere in Greek poetry, at 18.54, when the queen comes downstairs to talk with Odysseus in disguise as the beggar.[13] During the contest of the bow, Telemachus assumes the role of head male of the household, ordering his mother upstairs and speaking with authority to the suitors. All of this can be understood on the one hand as part of the maturing of Telemachus: he is supposed to learn about his father in order to be ready to help his father—or maybe even replace him. But in books 13–18, Telemachus is but one of several who stand in for Odysseus.

Theoclymenus, the mysterious prophet whom Telemachus meets by chance when he first arrives in Ithaka and then brings home with him, also has some interesting affinities to the absent king. He is a fugitive murderer, in exile from his home. Odysseus tells Athena in book 13 that he is a fugitive murderer, and he is, in any event, in exile from his rightful home. In contrast to both Telemachus and Eumaeus, Theoclymenus prophesies the imminent return of Odysseus, as does the disguised king on more than one occasion. Finally, Telemachus' adventures in the poem draw on an old folktale about the son who brings his father home from exile. Theoclymenus becomes in this sense the first version of Odysseus that his son restores.[14]

Eumaeus, too, takes the place of Odysseus in several ways. His outpost, with its careful husbandry, is a denatured residue of the regal order that once informed the palace in Ithaka.[15] While the suitors gobble up the substance of the royal household, Eumaeus tries to preserve some remnant of his master's goods in the countryside. When he drives off the dogs from the beggar, he foreshadows on a humble scale what Odysseus will do to the suitors; when Telemachus returns from his journey, Eumaeus greets him tearfully, "as a father kindly embraces his son . . ." (16.17–18). The swineherd is holding a place for his master from which Odysseus can begin to reclaim his property and his life as king. It is no accident that the poet has both the disguised king and his son start their returns with a visit to Eumaeus.

Books 13–17 feature, then, many approximations of Odysseus. As the hero makes his way toward the reckoning that will occur in the palace, his way is prepared by others, who place him within reach of the usurping suitors by proxy. And he will be there himself soon, first in the form of an apparently harmless beggar, then revealed in all his glory. So, too, the characters he himself creates in his false tales are approximations, having some things in common with the "real" Odysseus. The rover who speaks to Athena has been to Troy and returned with much plunder; he is suspicious and avoids exploitation by others through his wits; he was brought to Ithaka by others, whose ship was blown off course by storms; he arrived asleep, left onshore by his hosts along with his loot (13.256–86). With Eumaeus he is from a wealthy background, good at ambushes and raiding for plunder; a veteran of the Trojan campaign, he came home safely but then left to go raiding in Egypt; there his crew were destroyed by their own greed and lack of self-control, but he survived by making a friend of the king; he prospered there under the king's protection, then headed out for more plunder with a crew that proved both dishonest and greedy; they were killed by a storm at sea, but he survived, clinging to a single mast until he washed ashore among the Thesprotians and was again treated well by the king, who tried to send him home on a ship from his kingdom (14.192–359).

Our default assumption, especially when we are in the spirit of the *nostos* plot, is that the personae Odysseus creates in the countryside— and later for his own wife—are not "real." And yet parts of each story replicate the real adventures. How much needs to be changed before the true Odysseus becomes a fiction? What if we were to say that the false tales contain some elements that are false, some true, that the man we hear described is an altered version of the hero? Insofar as we assume that the personae are designed solely to help Odysseus manipulate others, these sorts of questions do not arise. The relationship forged in Eumaeus' hut is from this perspective also somehow not as real as, say, that between Odysseus and Alcinous because the swineherd is responding to "false" information about the stranger. There is, in effect, no real Odysseus for Eumaeus to know since that hero is presently stored away behind the disguise. But in thinking about a poem so self-conscious about the making of its own art, it is misleading to restrict ourselves to the perspective enforced by Athena and her imperatives.

THE (RE)MAKING OF ODYSSEUS

As Zeus says twice in the poem, Athena has arranged ahead of time for Odysseus to return home triumphant (5.22–24, 24.479–80). Her role as auteur of that scenario is enforced by the similes that describe her enhancing Odysseus' appearance like a silversmith creating a work of art (6.229–35; 23.156–62). The goddess, it is suggested, is in some sense the maker of the Odysseus who defeats the suitors and wins back his kingdom. Athena is not, of course, the only artist at work in the *Odyssey*. The bards Phemius and Demodocus both mirror Homer's own role as a creator of heroes through song.[16] But the most prominent narrative artist in the poem is Odysseus, who re-creates and reinforces his own *kleos* in books 9–12. There is, as we have said, no reason to doubt that he is basically telling the truth about what happened to him. There is also no doubt that he is using the stories to evoke a sympathetic response from his audience on Scheria, just as he does when speaking to Eumaeus. We might ask ourselves what the difference is between the stories in 9–12 and the "false tales." According to the rhetoric of the return plot, the former are first-person reports of things that actually happened while the latter are strategic lies.

But in a section of the story thick with models for Odysseus, a character who has been re-creating himself over and over throughout his long journey home, in a poem so attentive to the role of art in the creation of character, we could also see the false tales as part of a continuum along which various versions of Odysseus exist within the framework of the narrative.[17] There is a fluidity about the identities of all the characters we meet in this part of the poem, including Odysseus.[18] If we ignore for the moment Athena's controlling agenda, which tells us that in the case of her hero the fluidity is magical and unrelated to his identity, Odysseus' other selves fit seamlessly into the accommodating world of Eumaeus' rural outpost.

We may begin by observing that it is not unrealistic to wonder whether a man away from home and family for twenty years is in any sense the same person he was when he left. Nor is it surprising that such a man might himself wonder how or whether he can return home after so long. In this context, the false tales may be understood as a trying on of various personae, a cautious approach to reentry. And in any event, are the heroes of his two autobiographies or the idealized king of a settled kingdom more like the Odysseus who has spent at least half his life as a soldier and wanderer, living off the land and without fixed abode? Leaving aside the particulars, is the kind of man we meet in his stories obviously different from the hero of books 9–12? He says to Calypso that he yearns for his home and family, but the hero we have come to know in the first half of the poem fits the description in the yarn he tells Eumaeus pretty well (14.222–27):

> This was how I was in war. But working the land was never dear to
>   me,
> nor household chores, the husbandry that makes shining children.
> No, I loved always long-oared ships, and wars, sharp spears
> and well-polished arrows, dreadful things that other men
> found horrible; I loved them all—some god I suppose planted this
>   in me.

It is no accident that all of the stories we have about Odysseus after he returns from Troy have him leaving home and returning to the life of a wanderer.

CALYPSO REVISITED

Odysseus' self-creation reaches its most vivid expression in his false tales. In the previous adventures on his journey, he has encountered many different cultures and made his way repeatedly from stranger to celebrity. As these episodes unfold, we have begun to see a tension develop in the narrative between the goals of the return plot, always pursued and supported by Athena, and the actions of Odysseus, which sometimes seem to reflect a different set of assumptions about the significance of his actions and their relationship to his identity. This tension prompts, in turn, a reconsideration of some assumptions prompted by the Calypso episode. Because Athena effects his escape from Ogygia, her imperatives are aligned in that episode with the idea that in order to win *kleos,* and thus stay alive in an existential sense, the hero must reject the protection of the nymph and her timeless world in favor of the ordinary human world of death and change. The poet's repeated use of the imagery of rebirth in the Calypso episode and subsequent adventures further suggests that, once free, Odysseus continually re-creates himself by acting against the numbing effects of oblivion.

As we have seen, however, the connection between Athena's goals for Odysseus and his self-creation through action is made problematic as the story progresses. The poet's use of the participle *amphikalypsas* (5.493), an echo of the nymph's name, to describe Athena surrounding the hero with sleep when he arrives in Scheria is the first clue and prompts us to wonder whether the goddess's protection is entirely different from the nymph's. Later parallels implied between various "detaining women" and Penelope again cloud the distinction between the oblivion threatened by witches and the final rest in Ithaka. Although the goddess does free her favorite, it is not always clear that her plans for him are as different from Calypso's as they seem to be in book 5. She admires the qualities that allow him to manipulate others and work his will in the world of human action, but the triumph she arranges will place him in a situation uncomfortably similar to the otherworldly stasis he has been fighting against for ten years.

CONCLUSION

When Odysseus returns to Ithaka, we naturally feel a sense of anticipation: finally he is within striking distance of the obnoxious suitors. Athena is back on hand, ready to plot and scheme with her favorite. At this point the poet, true to his normal practice, teases us, slowing down the action and making us wait for the big finish. Insofar as we are swept up in the thirst for revenge, this delay is hard to endure, and this section of the poem has come in for criticism over the millennia. But if we look at the exchanges in the Ithakan countryside in the context of the evolving tension between competing visions in the poem, Eumaeus and various travelers who pass through this part of the story take on a richer coloration, playing their part in the articulation of the *Odyssey*'s complex meditation on the nature of human life.

First of all, we have seen in the encounters in Eumaeus' hut a continuation of the dynamic of the stranger who is not a stranger. Once again, Odysseus is anonymous, a nobody who happens to land on the doorstep of the kindly swineherd. As usual, we are in on the ruse, and so the conversation is filled with ironies. This much is familiar, as is the ease with which the unknown man can penetrate a new society and learn about its inhabitants. Indeed, Eumaeus recalls in many ways another independent herdsman living in a carefully managed space, Polyphemus. Both have heard that Odysseus might be coming, both play a part in the rebirth of the hero, and both are manipulated by "nobody." Of course, the contrasts are also striking: Eumaeus offers shelter and food from the master's precious herds, while Polyphemus plans to eat the master; the Cyclops lives without connection to his fellow monsters, and lacks any skills with which to form such relationships, while Eumaeus takes in the stranger and quickly forms a significant bond through the awareness of shared suffering. The key to the importance of Eumaeus lies in these differences.

The life stories that punctuate this section of the poem reflect in their own way the alternate visions of life we have been tracing. Odysseus' false tales show, on the one hand, his characteristic desire to control knowledge and use it to manipulate others. Keeping the swineherd at a distance allows the hero to assess his loyalty and control his behavior around the palace: no chance of him revealing too much at the wrong time. At the same time, the camaraderie that does develop between the two debased men, though based on "false" information about the wanderer, has an ease and immediacy not possible between a king and his servant. The relationship between Telemachus and Theoclymenus is a briefer version of the same dynamic: Telemachus, standing in, as does Eumaeus, for Odysseus as the head male of the household, takes in the young man in spite of his shady past and helps him find rest. And both of these hosts, in turn, find their counterparts in the kindly kings who populate Odysseus' false tales and Eumaeus' true one.

Although the validity of the personae Odysseus creates in his stories remains tantalizingly unresolved, the implications of these narrative acts for the larger thematic structure of the poem are clear enough. His autobiographies represent the most extreme expression of the impulse to self-creation that drives him all the way through the poem from nobody to Odysseus. In contrast to this sense of existential agency is the identity awaiting him in Ithaka, unchanging, realized through his assumption of various roles. Athena has been engineering his return, and her divine stamp is on the imperatives that sanction behavior painful and sometimes injurious to others. The world that this version of the hero will inhabit is magical, resistant, like the hero's identity, to the ravages of time, able to be restored in its entirety by the returned king.

By contrast, the nameless wanderer in Eumaeus' cloak moves through a world that is decidedly lacking in magic. There human life is pervaded by the operations of chance and the predations of time. No palace awaits him, no faithful wife and servants. He has no incentive to put off living until he gets home. Instead, he seizes the moment, forming a bond with the swineherd by swapping stories. His identity, though anchored by the history he details, is also formed through his interactions with others as they cross his path in the moment. Since he has little to lose, he need not guard his property, hiding it away in a cave or plotting slaughter to regain control of it. In the continuous arc of Odysseus' journey from Calypso to Ithaka—the poem's chronology, not the story's—this man represents a further step in the direction pointed by the anonymous strangers who arrived at Scheria, on the Cyclops' island, in the lair of Circe.

The narrative has come, in more than one sense, full circle. Odysseus has returned to Ithaka, whence he departed those many years before. But he also revisits here, in a different venue, the determination to immerse himself in the world of human mortality that drove him away from the nymph on Ogygia. Athena stands at his side, ready to effect his miraculous reincarnation as king, husband, father, and son. He, too, is ready, but the subversive part of his character, which sent him into the cave of Polyphemus, is also active, as if to answer the final push to reanimate him in the image of his prewar self.

The sojourn with Eumaeus is usually seen as an interlude that keeps Odysseus and us from the final reckoning with the suitors. But we can go beyond this assessment by asking what it is about the events between Odysseus' first landing on the beach and his eventual arrival in the palace in disguise—beyond the fact that they make us impatient—that prepares us for and enriches our appreciation of the poem's climax. The answer is that it is the stories that make this part of the poem important. The role of artful storytelling in the creation and preservation of human identity is a central theme in the *Odyssey,* and it finds unique expression here. The selves created in the encounters in books 13–16 come into being as the result not of command performances in a rich man's palace, full of glorious deeds reflecting regal status. Rather, the stories are given by men of humble means as reciprocal gifts, motivated by the impulse to share suffering, which binds all humans together, not to promote glory, which ensures their separation.[19]

Odysseus' false tales in particular focus the issues arising out of the tension, in the poem and in the character of its hero, between anonymity and celebrity, time and timelessness, mortal and immortal. These polarities will continue to inform the narrative as Odysseus finally reenters his home, penetrating the society of the suitors as a stranger. But before we return with him, there is one more lens through which we may look at his triumph.

Chapter Five

THE WARD OF HERMES

ODYSSEUS AS TRICKSTER

If Hermes is involved, after a touch of chaos comes a
new cosmos.

Lewis Hyde

The story of Odysseus' naming reveals a telling connection on his
mother's side of the family.[1] As the old nurse washes the beggar's
feet, she comes upon the scar (19.392–98):

> Right away she recognized
> the scar, a wound made long ago by a boar's white tusk
> when he went up Parnassos with Autolycus and his sons;
> Autolycus, his mother's worthy father, famed among men
> for thievery and false oaths. Hermes, the god himself, gave
> him these skills, delighted by thigh meat of lambs and kids
> the man burned for him. And the god was his ready partner.

As the disguised hero makes his way into the stronghold of the unsus-
pecting suitors, Homer links him to the premier trickster figure in Greek
myth.[2] We have seen how well Odysseus lives up to the name his grandfather gave him, bringing trouble to himself and others.[3] But the figure
of the trickster is more than a troublemaker. Crossing boundaries and

thereby blurring them, penetrating the precincts of the mighty, he disturbs the established order of things and makes room for creative change. In the view of the *nostos* plot, Odysseus infiltrates his own home to regain what was always rightfully his and by doing so reaffirms the proper order of things in Ithaka. But as always in this complex work of art, his actions have more than one meaning.

THE TRICKSTER

The figure of the trickster is ubiquitous, appearing in some form in Amerindian, Mediterranean, European, Asian, African, and other cultures. As with any such archetype, the variations between different realizations are of course significant, and generalizing can be misleading. Still, the figure does appear to retain some characteristics across cultures and time, as Lewis Hyde has recently shown.[4] We will not, in any event, be attempting an anthropological analysis of Odysseus as a trickster figure like Coyote in Native American folktales or even Hermes in the Greek tradition. Although the *Odyssey* came out of an oral tradition, its hero is a complex literary character drawn from many different paradigms, many of them remote from the trickster.

Yet there are some aspects of Odysseus' behavior on his return journey and within his own home that recall parts of the trickster paradigm, especially as it is realized by Hermes in the *Hymn to Hermes*.[5] What interests me in particular is how the trickster in his role as transgressor raises ontological issues, questions about "what is." Here is where the figure overlaps with the centrifugal Odysseus and his world. Seeing the hero from this perspective sheds light on the implications of his subversive behavior for the larger thematic structure of the poem.

The trickster's powers are almost always realized through motion. By crossing boundaries, he can blur the categories by which the world is understood, sometimes creating a fruitful chaos out of which new meaning is generated. Anytime a border is drawn, something must be excluded.[6] If the exclusion is absolute, the material bounded out is lost, and the result can be stasis and sterility. The trickster, by crossing, keeps the borders open, we might say. Lewis Hyde has called this kind of function "dirt work," in the sense that what is excluded becomes "dirt."[7] And, of course, what counts as dirt will vary according to one's view of how the world ought to be or is. As Hyde puts it, "If dirt is the by-product of the creation of order, then a fight about dirt is always a fight about how we have shaped our world."[8]

Here we encounter a dark potential by-product of exclusion, violence.[9] Once the shape of the world has been settled, those who benefit most from it become intent on preservation; what was once contingent and arbitrary becomes "natural," "true." Once the lines are drawn, guards appear to enforce them.

The trickster's motion, then, insofar as it is transgressive, can promote change. Since drawing boundaries around the flux of experience is one way to produce meaning, the one who crosses boundaries sees meaning as contingent, negotiable, not fixed. Likewise, within a milieu of permeable boundaries identity can also become fluid. Nor is it surprising that lying and thievery are both standard elements in the trickster's repertoire since each act challenges definitive boundaries, lying by challenging "the truth," stealing by challenging ownership.[10] Indeed, the two are related in that lying is a verbal analog to theft, an appropriation by which something "moves" from one meaning to another. Hyde takes this approach further by invoking the semiotic implications of motion.[11] That is, something can only signify by substituting for something else. Without motion, either in fact or in mind, meaning is not possible. We begin to see how it is that theft and/or lying can be the precondition to the creation of meaning.

Hyde cites two examples of motion as signification, both germane to our purposes: Tiresias' prophecy about Odysseus' final journey and Hermes' theft of Apollo's cattle in the Homeric *Hymn to Hermes*.[12] According to Tiresisas' prophecy in book 11, the oar on Odysseus' shoulder means one thing near the sea, another inland. What makes the difference is motion. Likewise, the cattle of Apollo, while they are undisturbed in the meadow, have no meaning in the mortal world: they are neither wild nor domestic; they do not reproduce, so their number remains fixed. Once Hermes moves them, they are sacrificed and become domestic as food, thus participating in death and change. We may add a third example, the Cattle of the Sun, which also have a fixed number, never dying or reproducing, and must never be disturbed—which is to say, moved.

One final point. The trickster figure is, with a few exceptions, male. The reasons for this aspect of the archetype are not entirely clear and are beyond the scope of our project here.[13] For our purposes, it is enough to note the phenomenon, which may have some implications for our understanding of how the trickster paradigm interacts with the articulation of Odysseus' character in the poem.

THE TRICKSTER AND THE HERO

Since Odysseus is often said to be the first comic hero in Western literature, we might well ask what the relationship is between that literary type and the folktale figure we call the trickster. In part this is a question of semantics, but there are also differences of function between the two types, and these are important for our purposes. First of all, the trickster is usually a supernatural being, capable of magical transformations, invisibility, and manipulation of the natural world, while the comic hero is usually mortal. But the more important distinction lies in the way each figure's acts affect the world in which he moves. Here the goals of the narrative are crucial. We tend to identify as comic certain kinds of stories that allow for a disruption of the regular order of things, with the understanding that the world will eventually be restored. We have said that the *nostos* plot of the *Odyssey* is driven by this assumption so that the poem is often called the first comic narrative in Western literature. Later examples include Greek Old and New Comedy (with certain of Euripides' romantic escape plays as possible predecessors), Roman Comedy, and Shakespeare's comic plays.

The key to the comic narrative is our trust that after disruption right order—however the narrative defines it—will be restored. We can enjoy all kinds of disorder if we know that the words and actions we are seeing are revocable. If our trust is betrayed, if the hero is murdered at the end of the story, we can feel cheated. The protagonist of a comic story is often deceptive, manipulating people and events within the world of the narrative to ensure the proper outcome. Because we want things to "come out right," we will forgive behavior that in other contexts might be distasteful or immoral. We recognize Odysseus in this description but also the clever slave of Plautine comedy or Shakespeare's Puck. And yet, despite the obvious overlap between this character type and the trickster, one crucial difference remains: the trickster is usually a force for change; the world is a different place when he leaves than when he came.

The trickster also shares some characteristics with the tragic hero in classical literature, a type with its origins in the Achilles of the *Iliad*. Here again the protagonist reflects the goals of the narrative. We call a story tragic, in a literary sense, when the goals of the narrative reinforce the need to accept limits on human action, the most important of these being death. Thus, unlike the comic world in which all is revocable, the tragic venue insists on a world of linear, irreversible time. Here words and deeds are irrevocable: "once blood is spilled, who can call it back?" says the chorus of Aeschylus' *Agamemnon* (1019–21). The typical tragic hero is unable to accept the fact of his own limitations, in particular his mortality, often behaving more like a god than a human. Sometimes the hero can eventually come to a new understanding of his place in the world, as does Achilles or Sophocles' Oedipus; sometimes, as with Sophocles' Ajax, he cannot, and the intransigence destroys him. In any event, the work of art impels us to this acceptance and shows us how the world changes when viewed from a perspective of humility.[14]

Like the trickster, the tragic hero is typically a liminal figure who can introduce new ideas and experiences into the established order as the result of his movement across significant boundaries. Tragic heroes often breach borders that are proof against lesser men, the trip to the underworld being the most common example. As a result of his journey, the hero brings back knowledge and experience unavailable to ordinary humanity. And by crossing boundaries, heroes help the rest of us understand where these dividing lines are and thus how the world is shaped. Achilles, having visited his own private underworld in response to the death of his friend Patroclus, suffers a profound change in his understanding of his place in the larger order of the cosmos. In the last book of the *Iliad,* he gives two speeches of consolation to Priam, the father of Hector.[15] The old man has come to beg the hero to release Hector's body for burial. Achilles attempts to console Priam for the loss of his son by urging him to remember that mortals are united in their suffering and powerlessness before the omnipotent gods: we must all accept whatever the gods give us and do the best we can with it. The humility exemplified here is worlds apart from Achilles' arrogant and selfish behavior earlier in the story. And because he has changed, we can share in his new wisdom.

Though both the tragic hero and the trickster can effect change, they differ sharply in their position in the world. While he has unusual abilities, the tragic hero, like his comic counterpart, is finally mortal, whereas the trickster is in some way beyond human status. The hero shows us the limits of human life precisely because he is himself mortal. Though often a loner, he is one of us. The trickster, by contrast, works from the margins, always an outsider. By intruding where he doesn't belong, he can disturb the world's shape, make meaning by making trouble. The hero is usually motivated by shame, whereas the trickster is essentially shameless; the hero may journey far from his home, but he can return there; the trickster has no home and is defined by motion and rootlessness.

HERMES

Hermes makes five significant appearances in the *Odyssey*. He carries Zeus' commands to Calypso in book 5; delivers the magic drug moly to Odysseus in book 10 to protect him from Circe's powers; leads the souls of the dead suitors to Hades in book 24; exchanges salacious remarks with Apollo in Demodocus' song about Hephaestus, Ares, and Aphrodite in book 8; and is named as the patron of Autolycus in the story of Odysseus' naming in book 19. The first three passages show the god in his role as the agent of Zeus and Athena, crossing boundaries but not subverting the established order of things. The conversation with Apollo places him within the inner circle of Olympians, though his appreciation of Aphrodite suggests a less reverent side of his character. Finally, the connection to Autolycus associates the god directly with subversion. As the agent of Zeus, Hermes supports Athena's plans for Odysseus in the context of the *nostos* plot. His powers of deception and manipulation may be reflected in the drug moly, but his mission places him firmly in support of the established Olympian order. The fullest expression of his trickster persona appears not in the *Odyssey* but in the later Homeric *Hymn to Hermes,* composed around 600–550 BCE. Here the patron of Autolycus comes into his own.

The *Hymn to Hermes* is basically the story of how an outsider becomes an insider. Hermes, we learn, was born in a cave in Arcadia far removed from the blessed gods on Olympus. His mother is Maia, a minor nymph, with whom Zeus has a brief but eventful fling—without, as usual, Hera's knowledge (1–9). The baby god is precocious, springing from his crib immediately and performing prodigious deeds on the first day of his life. He makes the first lyre from the shell of a tortoise, sings beautifully of his own birth, and steals the cattle of Apollo, driving the cattle backward and wearing strange sandals he has made from twigs to avoid detection. The ur–Boy Scout, he invents the method for making fire by rubbing sticks together and then sacrifices some of the cattle (22–154).

We see certain traditional aspects of the trickster here, deception chief among them but also transgressive motion and creativity. Hermes crosses more than one kind of boundary in the course of his adventures. He leaps from his mother's loins, moving from helpless infancy to self-sufficiency in an instant (20). He steps over the threshold of the "high-roofed cave" (23) and travels from Mount Cyllene to Pieria, penetrating the special precinct of the Olympians' sacred herds (72). He steals fifty head of Apollo's cattle and drives them across the river Alpheios into a new pasture and barn (99–108). After his sacrifice, he travels back home and slips through the keyhole of the cave's door "like an autumn breeze or a mist" (147).

The motion here is not simply physical. The baby god passes from the womb to full control of his powers, from the rural outlands of mortals into sacred Olympian space and then back again. He changes shape, from flesh to mist to flesh. He also acts as the agent for transformative change outside of himself. The lyre begins as a live tortoise, which Hermes addresses as "sexy curvy dancer" (31) before making it into an aesthetic artifact, moving it from the animal world into the realm of human culture. He drives the cattle of Apollo from the timeless, perfect existence of the gods into the mortal world of death and change. Even the sticks he uses to make fire move across the boundary between nature and culture. All of his creativity begins with some basic transformation, twigs into sandals, tortoise into lyre, sticks into fire.

In the aftermath of the theft, the poem's major themes emerge. Maia confronts her wayward son as he slips back into the crib, predicting dire consequences when Apollo discovers the theft. Hermes responds sharply: don't talk to me as if I were a little baby; I know what's best for us; we must be recognized as part of the inner circle of the Olympians, not continue living in some dark cave; Zeus had better give me the same honor as Apollo has or I'll become the king of thieves, breaking into Apollo's scared precincts at Delphi and stealing his tripods (163–81).

The theft of the cattle, it turns out, was designed to provoke Apollo and get the attention of Zeus. The rest of the story describes how Hermes achieves his goal, besting Apollo and gaining entrance to the Olympian regime. In the negotiations that effect this outcome, Hermes uses his invention, the lyre, as a bargaining chip, giving Apollo the instrument and, by implication, domain over the music it makes. He, meanwhile, invents the pipes and has his own music. Apollo, in return, makes Hermes the master of thieves, the lord over animals, and the patron of a rather obscure form of prophecy (254–580). As a result of the trickster's transgressions, the shape of the world has been changed. The boundaries that used to define the way things are have been breached and rendered porous. Lyres and pipes now make music, and sticks make fire. The baby god is now a part of the Olympian regime, and thievery becomes a part of the divine order.[16] Maia we do not hear of again, but we may suppose that her status rises with her son's.

Hermes in the hymn offers a good starting point for talking about Odysseus in the *Odyssey* because the hymn poet, like Homer, used folktale patterns to create a literary character. Much of what Hermes does in the course of the poem reflects the trickster, but finally the story has the shape of a rather supercharged bildungsroman, the growth of a young "boy" into maturity. Unlike the trickster, who has no home and wanders perpetually, Hermes finds himself a new home by moving up in the world. In this sense, the hymn, like the story of Autolycus in the *Odyssey*, supplies an earlier life history for a hero. The Hermes we see in the *Odyssey* is a tame version of the unruly infant of the hymn, his powers now entirely at the service of his father and the other Olympians. He has become what the return plot assumes Odysseus is, entirely *centripetal*.

That Odysseus often behaves like a trickster is not news.[17] The more important question is whether the archetype's appearance in the story adds anything to the articulation of the poem's reflections on human identity. We may begin by revisiting the adventures in books 5–12, where Odysseus passes through many different societies, none of which are to be his home. He is a wanderer, and like the trickster he sometimes brings about significant change.

KEEPING THE BOUNDARIES OPEN:
CALYPSO AND THE PHAEACIANS

As Odysseus moves from Ogygia to Scheria and thence to Ithaka, we see him slowly making his way back from a divine existence into the world of mortals. Stranded on the island of Calypso, the hero faces a pleasant but ultimately—from the point of view of human life—meaningless existence with the nymph. In this first appearance of Odysseus, the trickster paradigm is not obviously in evidence. Hermes, in his persona as a dutiful servant of Zeus, effects the release of Odysseus, who is in many ways as guileless as we will ever see him in the poem. His speech to the nymph is supremely tactful but basically truthful. Indeed, the power of the exchange comes from the emotional vulnerability in each of the characters. Still, the episode establishes a tension between the timeless perfection of the gods and the evanescent existence of mortals that will be definitive for the rest of the poem. Calypso's island vividly represents the kind of stasis that the trickster combats by penetrating its boundaries, keeping them open. Here Hermes plays the role of transgressor, effecting what will be for now Zeus and Athena's will, to release Odysseus into time. As we have seen, the differences between Calypso's oblivion and the blissful state that awaits the hero in Ithaka become less obvious as the poem progresses.[18] And as that gap closes, the trickster will appear to keep the way of escape open.

When he washes up on the shore of Scheria, Odysseus has moved toward the world of time and death but only partway. In their isolation, in their pursuit of pleasure and avoidance of pain, the Phaeacians live in a world far removed from the gritty reality of Ithaka. They are mortal but still closer to the gods than the protagonists who appear in the stories told in Eumaeus' hut. Odysseus has taken over from Hermes the role of boundary crosser now, and we begin to see the hero's manipulative, self-concealing side come to the fore. He plays on Nausicaa's naïveté and pubescent curiosity to get himself an audience before the queen. He withholds his name until he has won the admiration of the king, then enthralls the assembled crowd of admirers by telling the story of his long journey from Troy.

Storytelling can preserve *kleos.* By delivering his own version of the adventures, Odysseus joins the many others in the poem who preserve and augment his fame by telling stories about him.[19] At the same time, his performance has about it the air of enchantment, putting him in the company not only of bards such as Demodocus and Phemius, who sing the *klea andrôn,* but also of the antiheroic singers Calypso, Circe, and the Sirens. Lewis Hyde, speaking of the song that Hermes uses to enchant Apollo in the *Hymn to Hermes,* makes the connection:

Story and song: these are two of the hypnotics by which social orders maintain their self-enchantment, the radio playing all day in the laundries and gas stations, a background hum of catchy ballads to keep an agreed-upon reality in place and seemingly alive.[20]

Hyde's portrait of Hermes as trickster highlights the god's power to both enchant and disenchant. When he sings to Apollo in the hymn, he enchants; when he steals the cattle of Apollo, bringing them into time, he disenchants. The point is that, as one who works the boundaries, the trickster is neither enchanter or disenchanter alone but both at once:

He is neither the god of the door leading out nor the god of the door leading in—he is the god of the hinge. He is the mottled figure in the half-light . . . who simultaneously amazes *and* unamazes. . . . I sometimes wonder if all great creative minds do not participate in this double motion, humming a new and catchy theogony even as they demystify the gods their elders sang about.[21]

Odysseus tells his story to entertain the guests, to be sure, but perhaps also to strengthen the picture in their minds of himself as the invincible hero who must be returned to his rightful home. In other words, he is working to preserve the social world of the *nostos* with himself at the center, the king who can make everything right again if only he can get back to Ithaka.

POLYPHEMUS: MAKING THE WORLD WITH WORDS

The Cyclops episode always delights us because Odysseus uses words to rearrange the world, a typical ploy of the trickster: "Tricksters sometimes speak in a way that confuses the distinctions between lying and truthtelling or (to preserve the useful words "true" and "false") undercuts the current fictions by which the world is shaped."[22] The monster, we learn at the end of the episode, has been on the lookout for Odysseus (9.508–21):

Oh no! The ancient prophecy has come true! There was a seer, big
and tall, Telemus Eurymedes, who excelled at reading signs
and grew old telling prophecies among his fellow Cyclopes.

This man foretold it all, that I would lose my eye at the hands of
Odysseus. But I always looked for a big, handsome man to come,
wrapped in great strength. But now look, this feeble little wretch
got me drunk and robbed me of my eye!
But come here, Odysseus, so I can give you a guest-gift,
and ask famous Poseidon to grant you a safe journey.
For I am his son—at least he claims to be my father.
But if he pities me, he—no other god or man—will heal me.

We know well enough what the "guest-gift" will be. When Odysseus first
asked Polyphemus to honor the laws of hospitality sanctioned by Zeus,
the monster promptly ate two crew members, a grisly inversion typical of
his hospitality. In this place, being Odysseus would be dangerous. *Kleos,*
ordinarily the way to power, would here be an invitation to slaughter.

The famous pun that Odysseus uses nullifies this danger, changing
the shape of the world in the monster's cave.[23] By becoming *Outis,* "Nobody," he escapes the trap of fame (9.366, 403–12). Notice that the
reach of his verbal transformations extends beyond the monster. The
name *Outis* keeps the Cyclops from striking out against his adversary immediately, but it also implicates the rest of the island's inhabitants in his
scheme. The pun works because Odysseus enlists, without their knowledge, the other Cyclopes. "Nobody," who along with his anonymous
comrades should be helpless and alone in the cave, is suddenly allied
with the other monsters to further isolate his tormentor. And through
another pun, which links *mê tis* with *mêtis,* "intelligence," the world that
should be ruled by brute force is controlled instead by pure intelligence.

Odysseus uses more than one clever trick to escape, incapacitating
Polyphemus with wine and hiding the crew under the sheep to get them
past inspection at the mouth of the cave, but his use of words to manipulate reality is what makes everything else possible. We have said that
Odysseus is the principal agent of change in the poem. The trickster paradigm now gives us another perspective on this role. Everything about
the Cyclops initially urges us to see him as unsympathetic, an uncivilized
brute who kills without compunction. The same lens—through which we
look within the *nostos* plot—shows us Odysseus and his crew as victims.
But by the time Polyphemus loses his eye, our first impressions have
been shown to be inaccurate. The monster has been victimized by various tricks and isolated yet further than he already was, cut off from his

fellow Cyclopes by Odysseus' verbal manipulation of reality, completely blind instead of merely monocular. The shape of his world is forever changed by the transient trickster.

We have seen that in the other two large-scale adventures, the sojourn with Circe and the trip to the underworld, the threats to Odysseus, which bring out the trickster in him in other instances, are defused at the outset by Athena's agent Hermes. (Circe's advice to Odysseus, which keeps him safe in the underworld, may be seen as an extension of the leverage given the hero by Hermes.) In neither place do we see any permanent change as a result of Odysseus' presence. The Cattle of the Sun episode, which bears a strong resemblance to (and may have been a model for) Hermes' theft of Apollo's cattle, shows Odysseus in his centripetal persona, trying in vain to prevent the transgression, more reminiscent of Apollo than Hermes. The punishment of the Phaeacians by Poseidon, which immediately precedes Odysseus' arrival in Ithaka, can, on the other hand, be understood as part of the trickster paradigm. There, as in the Polyphemus episode, the boundaries of the world in which the natives live are penetrated by a deceptive traveler with the result that its peculiarities—which functioned well enough before—come into contact with a reality from without and harden into something permanently painful.

The relationship between the trickster paradigm and the *nostos* plot oscillates between two poles in these episodes, creating what Hyde calls a double movement. The Nobody of the Cyclops tale is closely allied with Odysseus in his centrifugal persona, while the stories the hero tells about himself among the Phaeacians support the goals of the *nostos*. Odysseus, like Hermes, can both enchant and disenchant, can create new worlds through his words and also call the reality of established ones into question by widening our perspective. We will see this double movement throughout the second half of the *Odyssey*. The hero returns to reaffirm the unchanging status that Athena works to preserve, while the trickster keeps the boundaries that define the world of Ithaka open.

EUMAEUS AND THE TRICKSTER

The double movement of Odysseus intensifies once he returns to Ithaka. Now we are primed for the pleasures of Athena's plan, the pitiless retribution, the loutish villains brought low. Disguised, the hero stalks his prey, aided by his adoring son and retainers, even the goddess herself. Once he gets home again, we feel, all will be as it should be. Meanwhile, the old beggar creates other lives for Odysseus, lives less focused on his wife, family, and estates, drawn rather to the excitement of wandering brigandage. Here the trickster as storyteller comes forward.

The return plot implies an Odysseus unchanged by time and circumstance. Under the wrinkles and dirty clothes, the king, with hair like curling hyacinths and the strength of youth, waits to take his revenge. Indeed, he lives only to regain what has been unfairly usurped. He longs for his home and family, and nothing will stop him from returning. His realm also has about it, in this perspective, something magical like Olympus. We are urged to follow Athena's lead in feeling indignant that such a place should be sullied by the gluttonous excesses of the suitors. But, as we have seen, the stories that Odysseus tells to Athena, Eumaeus, and later Penelope show us a very different man. The beggar is definitely beaten down by life's difficulties and has the wrinkles to show for it. He is no king and can gain entrance to palaces only if invited out of pity. This man has no established home, no family waiting to welcome him back. This is just as well because he doesn't like staying home, preferring wandering, war, and piracy to domestic tranquillity.

What the beggar is showing Eumaeus—and us—is in part what a man like Odysseus, who has gone through what Odysseus has, might well have become—might have become, that is, if the boundaries that shape the heroic return were a little more porous. Structures, as we have said, require boundaries, which legislate exclusion. One way to understand the character that Odysseus creates through narrative in the second half of the *Odyssey* is as a kind of antitype to the single-minded, focused hero of Athena's *nostos*. That character is bounded by his desire—echoed on the divine level by Athena's will—to restore the world as it was when he left for Troy. As he draws closer to the palace, the demands of the plotting he and Athena do grow more insistent: timing is everything; everyone in Ithaka must be controlled and made to play his or her proper part in the restoration. The boundaries are growing yet more restricted. As if in response to that tightening, Odysseus' other selves come to the fore in his stories. The trickster leads us across the boundaries and shows us other possible lives, revealing a fullness in the universe that the return plot tries to keep out. If Athena's king has not been affected by age and circumstance, the beggar will keep the way open for the passage of time and the quirks of fortune. If Odysseus is more like a god than a man, the beggar will remind us of the frailty of mortals and the existence they lead.

It is part of the richness of the *Odyssey* as a work of art that both ways of seeing the world are served by the figure of the disguised beggar. He is Athena's creation, just as is the beautiful Odysseus who dazzles Nausicaa and Penelope, and his persona allows him to work his heroic will on the suitors. At the same time, he embodies one form of the subversive, antiheroic wanderer who reflects much of what Odysseus actually does on his way home as opposed to what he professes to be. The double motion of the trickster, as enchanter and disenchanter, comes to fruition in Odysseus' autobiographical narratives. For the Phaeacians he tells a story that enchants, that preserves and augments his regal, godlike nature; for Eumaeus, he creates a character who would disenchant the magical narrative of Athena.

CONCLUSION: ODYSSEUS AT THE THRESHOLD

We have seen that the trickster often deals with a society's dirt, with what is excluded when the boundaries that define a group and its world are drawn. It is perhaps not surprising, then, that we find Odysseus playing the trickster at Eumaeus' outpost, appearing as a marginal—shall we say "liminal"?—figure, someone who has gotten his hands dirty in the course of his life. Eumaeus himself might well be understood as one of the excluded, no longer a part of the established order of things in the debased kingdom of his former master. (Perhaps, too, the strange interview with Laertes in book 24 shows us Odysseus working slyly on the margin as a trickster, in the dirt with his debased father—but more about that in the next chapter.)

We have also said that the trickster is usually implicated in the shape of "what is" because of his transgressive motion. So Odysseus, when he enters the persona of the trickster, can change "what is" on Scheria, in the cave of the Cyclops, perhaps even in the heart of the nymph Calypso. His greatest challenge, as an agent of change, is to drive out the suitors, to change the shape of things in his own home. Here we arrive yet again at the central tension in the poem expressed through various polarities, time/timelessness, stasis/change, mortal/divine. Are we to understand what happens in books 17–24 as a changing *back,* the reestablishment of what was, held in abeyance while the king was away, or a new world accommodated to the changes brought on by the passage of years? And who exactly returns? Is it Odysseus the godlike hero, untouched by the ravages of time, driven only by his desire to reach the center of his existence in the bed anchored by Athena's olive tree, or another kind of man, marked by his past, the product of the imposition of his remarkable will on the world around him, restless and hungry for experience to validate his existence?

Chapter Six

SLEEPERS AWAKE

THE RETURN OF THE BEGGAR

The *Odyssey* begins with the question: where is Odysseus? As the story unfolds, a second, more difficult quandary surfaces: who is Odysseus? By the time the disguised hero reaches the threshold of his palace, the first mystery seems to have been solved but not the second. Indeed, it appears that the two may be related in ways not obvious at the beginning of the poem and that the first is more complex than we may have originally supposed. The enduring hold on our imagination, of the *Odyssey* as a poem and Odysseus as a character, can be traced to the issues that arise when we ask these two questions. And because we experience so much of the story through the eyes of its principal protagonist, to answer them is to confront the central meaning of the poem. Only at the end of the narrative do we have all that Homer offers us by way of answers.

I suggested in chapter 2 that the dissatisfaction many have felt about the end of the *Odyssey* has to do with the imperfect fit between the hero that the *nostos* plot requires and the man we have seen evolving in the previous twenty-two books of the poem. Having traced the emergence of the stranger and the trickster in the story, we are now in a position to explore in more depth the implications of the tensions between centripetal and centrifugal forces in the poem and its hero. Rather than seeing the centrifugal aspects of the character simply as failures of self-discipline or excusable naughtiness reflecting a double standard in the society out of which the poem emerged, we may now consider them as representations of an alternative way of understanding the hero and his mission. To put it another way, we now have a way of telling the story that is more detached from the imperatives of Athena's perspective.

In response to the beggar, Penelope emerges from her quiescence in last third of the poem, stepping forward just in time to offer her husband unwitting support but also some cause for anxiety. The "like-mindedness" that she and Odysseus exhibit may also be understood in the light of our dual perspective.

THE MALE LIBERATOR

One experience recurs often for those who would work out the internal logic of the *Odyssey:* tracing consistent patterns of action throughout the journey from Troy to Ithaka, they seem to find themselves in an interpretive cul-de-sac when the patterns reappear in the poem's climax and inconveniently undermine our confidence in the finality of the hero's restoration. We have noted, for instance, how often Odysseus enters a space that is somehow feminized and then, by exerting his masculinity, effects his release from a stasis associated with the feminine aspects of the place. The pattern begins in the poem with Hermes in the role of the male liberator, effecting the release of Odysseus from Calypso's island. From then on, Odysseus becomes his own liberator. The island of the Phaeacians, the cave of Polyphemus, the island of Circe, and the underworld are all feminized places from which Odysseus must free himself. We further observe that Ithaka has been defined from the beginning of the poem by its lack of masculine authority: the suitors are the moral equivalent of children;[1] the atmosphere in the palace is characterized by a passivity and impotence that the heroic world, at least, associates with mortal women.

At this point, following the return plot, we encounter some interesting questions. If Ithaka does indeed fit the model of the feminized space threatening to Odysseus, then what would it mean for Odysseus to be "freed" from Ithaka? Who is the liberator and who is to be liberated? We may, of course, simply declare that Ithaka, because it is the goal of the return, is different from all the other places. But other answers might well be possible even if we do not exempt Ithaka. Perhaps the beggar is the version of Odysseus to be freed and the returning hero is the liberator. In this perspective, the handing over of the bow is the crucial moment when the hero reappears and the beggar is saved. We may further say that Telemachus' agency in the return is made yet more vivid in this view: he becomes, at the moment he hands the bow to the beggar, the son who brings his father back from exile, a traditional folktale pattern we have seen foreshadowed in the figure of Theoclymenus. Or could we say that the version of Odysseus to be freed—following the model of a realm immune from change—is some version of the king who went to Troy twenty years before magically preserved and ready to reappear?

Both of these interpretations are possible, but they do not exhaust the possibilities. What if we were to pursue the *nostos* pattern's usual implications? The Odysseus released might also be the centrifugal hero, who needs to keep moving to remain himself. From what is he to be released? From the stasis implied by the center he is supposed to be seeking. Here the prophecy of Tiresias, which Odysseus relates to his wife on their first night together, takes on a new tonality. The hero, feeling the fearful power of the center, breaks gently to his wife the necessity for more traveling.

These issues take us to yet another intriguing figure, the detaining woman. Odysseus has been threatened by female forces of all kinds in the poem: Calypso, Nausicaa, Circe, the Sirens. All would keep him from completing his mission. The divine versions hold out a special form of oblivion, an eternal bliss outside of human time. And, as we learned in book 5, memory exists only in time and is a prerequisite to *kleos*, which guarantees heroic identity and so forth.[2] Yet Penelope, the only candidate for the detaining woman in Ithaka, we exclude from consideration because she is part of what he would be detained from reaching.

But again, this exclusion is part of the magical return plot. In this view, Penelope embodies the imperative for Odysseus to cease wandering, to settle down; she is the center toward which he struggles. Again we might say that while the state of motionlessness is equated with death everywhere else in the poem, Ithaka is different. Here the poet's sleight of hand in the Calypso episode becomes clear once more. Penelope and the world Odysseus would live in with her are presented in book 5 as the complete antithesis of Ogygia, when in fact we will subsequently find many parallels between Odysseus' wife and all the detaining women in the poem. The final recognition scene between husband and wife underscores, as we have seen, the agency of Athena in pressing Odysseus' claims. She beautifies him as she does before he meets Nausicaa; he is bathed—always dangerous for the male hero—and loses control in the presence of his wife. Again we need to invoke the exemption. There is no analogous threat here: Penelope is different.

Widening our perspective in this way has implications for our understanding of Penelope.[3] Seeing Penelope as a detaining woman prompts some contradictions in the context of current debates about her status in the poem. On the one hand, she becomes invested with a certain degree of power in the life of Odysseus that the perfectly faithful wife does not have. At the same time, she is placed in opposition to what might be called Odysseus' "best interests" as the *nostos* plot sees them: she is an obstacle to the fulfillment of his mission. And yet—a further complication—Penelope can only be a detaining woman for the centrifugal Odysseus, and his mission in this view is not to reach home but to do something else involving motion that would allow him to become—what? a self-created man in the existential sense?

THE STRANGER

As the beggar, Odysseus exemplifies the stranger who is not a stranger in its richest form. Anonymous, he easily gains entrance to a place where, as Odysseus, he would be in great danger. In this sense, he reprises the role of "Nobody" in the Cyclops episode. And certainly *mêtis* is at work here in many forms. All of this is entirely consistent with the imperatives of the *nostos* plot. Likewise, as a stranger Odysseus certainly delivers to Ithaka, as to other places he has entered anonymously, suffering and death. Of course, those who are punished in book 22 deserve it according to Athena. This brings us to the intriguing figure of Amphinomos, the "good suitor."[4] The poet takes pains to distinguish this character from the general run of the suitors. He has stayed around, to be sure, eating the food and perhaps sleeping with the maids, but he also urges the suitors not to murder Telemachus (16.406) and protects the beggar and the servants in the palace from abuse (18.412).

In response to Amphinomos' kind treatment of him, the beggar offers wisdom won through suffering and then a warning. The young man seems to be sensible—the beggar knew his father. Attend then, he says, to this (18.130–42):

The earth nourishes nothing more frail,
of all that creep and breathe in this world,
than humans. A man never believes he'll suffer,
as long as the gods give him power, and his knees
hold their spring. But when the immortals bring pains,
then he must bear them, though unwilling,
in his enduring heart.
For such is the mind of mortal creatures,
as the father of gods and humans brings, day by day.
I was once destined to be fortunate among men,
and made much wickedness, relying on my strength,
trusting in my brothers and my father.
And now look. Let no man trample on the laws,
but receive in silence what the gods give.

The beggar goes on to say that the king, whose stores Amphinomos and his fellow suitors are wasting, is close by and will return soon. He should leave now while he has the chance. But Amphinomos, the poet tells us, "would not escape his fate." Athena had already "bound him" to die at Telemachus' hands (18.155–56).

The character of Amphinomos seems to exist in the story only to highlight the unrelenting vengeance of Athena. Here is an apparent anomaly among the selfish, greedy suitors, someone who can see the suffering of others and empathize with them. Surely he could be spared? No, in the triumphalist vision of Athena, all the suitors must die. Like all gods, she wants what she wants, and no delicate moral scruples will stand in the way. By contrast, the beggar's speech, as Murnaghan has noted, epitomizes the vision of human life opposed in the poem to that of the return plot: let no man (even Odysseus) assume that the gods will always make the sun shine on him; pain and misfortune come for us all. These thoughts are exactly those of Achilles in *Iliad* 24, when he finally lets go of his godlike anger and arrogance, reaching out to comfort Priam, a fellow mortal in pain.

The spirit of these words is also that of the stories told at Eumaeus' outpost. In the face of human suffering, the appropriate response is compassion, not self-righteous condemnation. As hero, Odysseus considers the suitors worthy of immediate death; as beggar, he makes a fleeting connection with one member of a group and tries to save him from the hero. The momentum of the revenge plot can make us forget that many of these young men are locals whose families Odysseus would have known all his life. But the hero is immune from any feelings of connection. Only as a nameless beggar can he draw on a reservoir of compassion in himself.[5] As was the case all along the journey home, anonymity fosters openness and connection while *kleos*, the measure of heroic stature, isolates. In the exchange between Amphinomos and the beggar, we are given a brief glimpse past the tight boundaries of Athena's plot to the wider world kept alive in the Ithakan countryside.

TRICKSTER

Of the trickster in Native American folktales, Mac Linscott Ricketts has observed:

> The trickster . . . embodies [an] experience of Reality . . . in which humans feel themselves to be self-sufficient beings for whom the supernatural spirits are powers not to be worshipped, but ignored, to be overcome, or in the last analysis mocked.[6]

Traditions vary as to how they realize any archetype, and the overlap between Greek and Native American cultures is not great. Nevertheless, Ricketts' observation points to a significant aspect of the fundamental tension between centripetal and centrifugal in the *Odyssey*. While the centrifugal version of Odysseus hardly mocks or ignores the power of the gods, neither does he look to them as the final guarantors of his identity or his destiny. The relationship between human and divine reality is always complex in Greek literature, and the *Odyssey* is no exception.[7] Still, as the slaughter of the suitors draws near, the tensions in the narrative focus insistently on the divide between mortal and immortal. The hero Athena creates and restores to power reflects her divinity. But he also is shadowed by another figure, mortal, anonymous, transient, open to a wider field of experience than the triumphant king. This latter figure, like the trickster, sees himself as the product of his own will, not as part of a larger, divinely controlled plan. He is born, in this sense, on Calypso's island when he refuses Calypso's offer of immortality.

We have seen that the trickster, by crossing boundaries, keeps them open and thus combats the stasis and sterility that can come with exclusive purity. At the end of the *Odyssey,* the potential for stasis resides in the magical vision of Athena, asserting a kingdom that does not acknowledge the passing of time. And of course, that vision entails violence: the true king of Ithaka must prevail; no exceptions can be made, no dirt allowed inside the pure space.[8] The beggar, in his role as trickster, represents the subversive dirt worker, keeping the boundaries porous. Athena's magical dispensation would cancel out time, asserting a kind of immortality for the restored realm of her favorite: son, wife, and father all in place, loyal servants at the ready. As he does elsewhere, Odysseus in his trickster mode presses the society of Ithaka toward change, a realization of what has been only potential. In this case, as on the island of the Phaeacians, the transient pushes the society to face the implications of its exclusions: twenty years have passed, the king has grown older, his father is dying, his son has grown up—and his wife may be nearing the end of her endurance.

The stringing of the bow, as it relates to the return of the hero, brings into sharp focus, as we have said, these two opposing visions of time. The contest sets in motion the eventual slaughter of the suitors while at the same time seeming to settle once and for all the question of who will be the head male in Ithaka. The linear, evolutionary story of Telemachus' journey to manhood, which began in books 1–4, stops abruptly here, colliding with the circular return plot. To put it another way, Odysseus' nod stops time, asserting the primacy of restoration over change.[9] From this perspective, the moment is parallel to the poem's conclusion, when Athena arbitrarily steps in and halts the impending battle between Odysseus and his family on one side and the families of the suitors on the other.

The strange reunion of Odysseus and Laertes may also reflect obliquely the subversive trickster. Odysseus finds the old man out in the country. He debates with himself whether to tell his father the "truth"— that his son has returned to rule the kingdom just as he did twenty years before—or to test him. His choice has always seemed pointlessly cruel: he tells the old man that he saw Odysseus once five years before but never again. He and we then watch as Laertes sinks into the dirt. But if the inner debate of Odysseus reflects the ongoing tension in the poem, then what he tells his father is not just a malicious lie but a glimpse at the other world that Athena would negate, a world in which the passage of time brings change. He becomes, one more time, a homeless wanderer.

By sinking into the dirt, Laertes acts out what this vision implies, moving toward the material excluded by magic from Ithaka.

PENELOPE

What we have been saying about the trickster has major implications for the portrait of Penelope.[10] However we choose to interpret her actions in the last six books of the poem—a choice that has inspired some warm debates over the millennia—it is generally agreed that her decision to show herself before the suitors in book 18 marks a major turning point in the presentation of this complex and enigmatic figure (18.158–62):[11]

> In the mind of Penelope, Ikarios' prudent daughter,
> the gray-eyed goddess Athena placed the urge
> to show herself to the suitors, so she might stir up
> their hearts and become more honored than before
> by her husband and son.

Until this moment, Penelope has been largely a passive spectator, coming down the stairs to speak briefly to her son or the suitors, returning to her bedroom to weep. She held the suitors off with the trick of the shroud but was eventually found out, so the pressure is mounting for her to remarry. She is initially nonplussed by the inner prompting and laughs *achreion,* "foolishly," or perhaps "with embarrassment."[12] She then tells her maid Eurynome of the impulse (18.164–69):

> Eurynome, my heart prompts me, for the first time,
> to show myself to the suitors, though they are hateful to me.
> I would say a word to my son, too, that would profit him.
> I'd tell him not to mix with the arrogant suitors,
> who seem friendly now but plot evil later.

The maid agrees that Penelope should warn Telemachus, but first she should bathe and put on some makeup. She should not go before the men with tearstained cheeks: mourning makes things worse (18.170–74). Penelope rejects the advice, saying that the gods took away all of her beauty when Odysseus left for Troy, and asks two of her attendants to accompany her downstairs so that she will not seem forward. The maid bus-

tles off, but Athena has other plans, putting Penelope to sleep and beau-
tifying her with divine ambrosia, making her appear taller and "whiter
than sawn ivory" (18.185–96).

The appearance has a powerful effect on the suitors. Eurymachus
speaks for the group in praising her beauty, a remark that prompts her
to repeat what she said to Eurynome about the gods taking away her
beauty. Then comes her report of what Odysseus told her before he left:
if Telemachus has reached manhood (when he has a beard) and he has
not yet returned, she should choose a new husband. That time has arrived, she says, and though remarriage is hateful to her, it must soon
come. She then suggests that gifts are usually a part of the prospective
groom's approach, and the hall is soon filled to overflowing with offer-
ings from the suitors, who clearly sense, as has the maid, that Penelope is
moving toward a decision to remarry. Meanwhile Odysseus, looking on
at this performance by his wife, is delighted to see her soliciting gifts with
sweet talk while having—he assumes—another intention in her mind
(18.243–84). Although she does not settle on the contest of the bow until her conversation the following evening with the beggar, Penelope
seems to begin the process here that leads to the slaughter of the suitors
and the return of her husband.

Most of the controversy about Penelope over the centuries has begun
with the assumption that, in spite of enormous pressure from the suitors
and the uncertainty about Odysseus' return, her loyalty to the king turns
out to be beyond question.[13] She loves Odysseus and will remain faithful
to him at least until his death is certain. What we don't know is whether
she can hold off the suitors long enough to be sure one way or the other.
Not surprisingly, the issue of Penelope's autonomy and agency has come
to the fore in the last thirty years or so, reflecting the rise in feminist
scholarship on the *Odyssey*. What does she know and when does she know
it? Is she in on the plot with Odysseus from the time he meets her disguised as a beggar or does she somehow do the right thing without knowing it? To what extent is she controlled by Athena? By tricking him into
losing his composure in book 23, does she beat Odysseus at his own
game?

Though this is not the place for a full-scale review of these complex issues, our approach will prompt further questions about the queen in the
course of this last look at the poem's conclusion. The return plot derives
much of its urgency from the threat of disloyalty implied by the story of

Agamemnon's disastrous homecoming.[14] In this view, Penelope is never completely to be trusted, and so she is kept in the dark about the plans to murder the suitors. Though admired for her loyalty, she is not in any sense presumed to be Odysseus' equal. It is understood in this view that Athena is the real agent of the queen's sudden decision to show herself to the suitors. For Athena, Penelope is, like every other character except Odysseus (and even he is not always in the know),[15] a tool to be used for effecting her plans. She is a goal to be reached, not a person with desires and priorities of her own. So the goddess makes Odysseus' wife enflame the suitors so that she will look better to her husband. He, meanwhile, is confident that, though she seems to be flirting, she has other intentions.

It has been noted, on the other hand, that the kind of psychic intervention Athena makes in book 18 is not usually understood as representing ideas and/or impulses completely foreign to the mortal involved. Rather, when a deity puts something into the mind of some man or woman, the result is to stir emotions or ideas already present on some level in the recipient of the stirring.[16] Thus Penelope's impulse to show herself to the suitors, though prompted by Athena, also realizes some emotion already present in the queen. I have suggested elsewhere that the portrait of Penelope here draws on that of Nausicaa earlier, that the picture of awakening emotions in the adolescent is transformed into an analogous stirring of long-dormant urges in the older woman.[17]

Penelope's state of mind prior to book 18 has been described as resembling a "frozen grief."[18] The analogy is apt. One of the characteristics of grieving figures, in Greek literature and subsequently, is the desire to stop time, to fight against the need to accept loss and rejoin the stream of life.[19] The ruse of the shroud is typical in this respect: completion implies readiness for the death of Laertes and the inexorable forward motion of time.[20] By unraveling her work, Penelope tries to hold back time, to stay in a state of suspended animation until Odysseus returns. This impulse, of course, parallels Athena's willed suspension of time in the *nostos* plot. When Penelope questions the beggar in book 19 and he says that he met Odysseus in Crete just before the latter set off for Troy, her emotions overflow (19.203–9):

He spoke, telling many lies that were like truth.
And as she listened, tears began to flow, softening her complexion.
As when snow melts on peaks of the mountains,

snow that the West wind piles up and the East wind thaws,
and the rivers overflow with its melting.
So her lovely cheeks were softened with the running tears,
as she wept for her husband, who was sitting beside her.

This beautiful simile makes explicit what the impulse to show herself to the suitors marks implicitly, the beginning of a thaw, as Penelope's feelings break loose and begin to sweep her toward the decision to hold the contest of the bow.

The question of whether Penelope sets up the contest because she senses on some level that the beggar is Odysseus and intuits the need to forward his plans or because in fact she finally gives up hope and resigns herself to remarriage to someone else can never be answered definitively. Likewise, the degree to which the queen acts as her own agent, as opposed to the instrument of Athena, is irresolvable. Scholars like to tidy up these kinds of ambiguities, but storytellers do not. The more room for doubt, the more the audience can participate in the creation of the poem's meaning. What we can say is that the scene between the beggar and the queen, and, indeed, the entire presentation of Penelope in books 18–23, hardly suggests someone acting like a robot. Passionate, stubborn, resourceful, she seems to find her own way to the decision that sets the slaughter of the suitors in motion.

We should hardly be surprised to find the characterization of Penelope ambiguous given the tension we have been tracing in the poem. Indeed, the poles between which the portrait oscillates reflect that tension while complicating our understanding of the character yet further. In the perspective of the *nostos* plot, we see a desirable woman potentially vulnerable, as Clytemnestra was, to the blandishments of suitors. Thus, though she may well be entirely faithful, this Penelope cannot be trusted and must be kept ignorant of her husband's return until the work of revenge is done. Likewise, her awakening must be seen as somehow manageable by the goddess and her mortal favorite. And yet the queen who awakens in book 18, speaks to the beggar alone, and then sets up the contest of the bow appears to be fully alive within the world of the centrifugal Odysseus, torn by the imperatives of time and the vagaries of fortune, ready to move on with her life no matter how painful the prospects appear. In short, a dangerous woman to have on the loose.

But if the world of the beggar, within which the exchanges in the countryside occur, is still alive in the poem, then we may see Penelope's assertiveness in yet another way. In contrast to the weeping passivity of book 1, when she tries to silence the bard and avoid the pain of thinking about her husband (1.328–44), her curiosity leads her to seek out the beggar after appearing before the suitors in book 18 to find out what he knows about Odysseus. And, although she is a queen, she has no trouble forming a bond with the ragged old man, reflecting the liberating fluidity offered to those who open themselves to the wider range of human experience that the beggar represents. Again, we may see the entire interview as orchestrated by the goddess, and if so we try to understand the queen's decision to hold the contest of the bow as a response to the manipulation of the disguised Odysseus.[21] Both perspectives are available.

We can, in fact, observe a kind of alternation in Penelope's behavior in books 18–23, a portrait of her own struggle to accommodate the disturbing feelings that begin to surface as the beggar draws near. In books 1–17, she remains essentially consistent with the goals of the *nostos* plot, passive and loyal. Her response to the promptings of her heart in book 18 shows her swinging back and forth between the desire to remain in stasis and the urge to break out of her suspended animation: her heart urges her, she claims that her beauty is gone; Athena makes her desirable, she awakens and prays to Artemis to kill her; Eurymachus praises her beauty, she denies it; she coyly solicits gifts and talks of remarrying, then goes back upstairs with her maids. Later, in the interview with the beggar, she denies again that she is desirable, using the same language she did with the suitors. But eventually she reveals to the beggar her strange dream, in which she says her pet geese—surely a symbol of the suitors—are slaughtered by an eagle, and she mourns for her loss. The feelings revealed here are unmistakable, an attachment to the men who flock around her. Her decision to set up the contest of the bow follows shortly, as if to make concrete the implications of her new awakening.

The exchanges between Penelope and Telemachus track the ambiguity in another way.[22] When he returns to Ithaka in book 17 with Theoclymenus, his mother eagerly asks what he learned about Odysseus. He sends her back upstairs to bathe and dress, showing an air of command commensurate with his new maturity. She complies, lapsing into the silent, passive woman we have come to know (17.41–56). This kind of exchange recurs more than once in the remaining episodes of the poem. Telemachus sends his mother away at the beginning of the contest of the bow (21.344–53) and rebukes her after the slaughter when she does not immediately accept Odysseus back into her arms (23.97–103). Each time, the queen obeys her son without complaint, the compliant wife of the *nostos* plot. But of course, the assertiveness in Telemachus reflects his readiness to take over as head male, something not in Athena's plan. These tensions reach a crescendo in the final recognition scene between husband and wife to which we now return.

RECOGNITION

Book 23 opens with Penelope back up in her bedroom, asleep, or perhaps we should say seeking oblivion, opting out of time until her husband returns. She has been there—weeping for Odysseus, then put to sleep by Athena—since Telemachus ordered her out of the hall before the beggar got control of the bow. The old nurse awakens her with the exciting news that Odysseus is indeed back and has killed all the suitors. The queen is not only unconvinced but annoyed. She hasn't had such a good sleep since before her husband left for Troy. Why is she now disturbed with such a crazy story (23.1–24)? The moment has occurred before: when she awakens after being beautified by Athena in book 18, she wishes Artemis would prolong her unconsciousness by killing her (18.201–5); as Odysseus falls asleep on the night before the great slaughter, she awakens and again prays to Artemis to bring her permanent oblivion with her gentle arrows (20.61–65). We should note that in book 18 and here again in book 23, the verb Penelope uses to describe the onset of sleep is *kalyptô:* "what a soft sleep covered me over" (*kalypsen,* 18.201); "why did you wake me from sweet sleep, which bound me, covering over (*amphikalypsas*) my eyelids?" (23.17). Part of Penelope wants to be with Calypso, out of time, away from pain. Indeed, seen through the lens of the centrifugal hero, she *is* the nymph.

Eurykleia persists, and Penelope begins to hope. Could it be true? But how could he, one man, kill all those suitors? The nurse only knows that the hall is full of corpses and Odysseus lives. Penelope is not yet convinced. This is not the time for crowing, she tells the old servant. It must be a god who killed them. Odysseus is still far away, dead (23.25–68). The wavering in the queen is expressed here, as elsewhere, in terms of sleep and wakefulness—or, in the standard analogy of the Greek imagination, death and life. We think again of the underworld, with all of its dead women forsaken by heroic or divine husbands. And killing the suitors, we are reminded, is the magical work of Athena's godlike favorite.

Eurykleia finally manages to get the queen down to the hall to see for herself. She ponders, as Odysseus will later do in the presence of Laertes (23.87–88):

> ... should she question her dear husband from afar,
> or go to him, kiss his head and hold his hands?

She remains aloof, looking at the old beggar, who sometimes reminds her of Odysseus, but then reverts to the bloody, ragged figure of the stranger. Telemachus is angered by her reticence: why doesn't she go to her husband? Her heart is made of stone. She patiently explains that she is still stunned by it all, but if it really is Odysseus then she and he will easily know each other. They have secret signs, hidden from all others. Odysseus now intervenes, urging his son to let Penelope test him. She will recognize him soon enough. Now he is filthy and dressed in rags, so she cannot know him. Meanwhile, they should clean up and attend to practical matters (23.97–122). Various perspectives coexist here. Penelope wonders whether she is looking at an old beggar or Odysseus. Telemachus, loyal son that he is, only wants her to see the conquering hero he has been waiting for. With the poem's contending visions in mind, we might rephrase her dilemma: which Odysseus is she seeing?[23]

The queen's suggestion that the matter of the beggar's identity could be settled between the two of them by reference to private, secret signs brings back the Penelope who manipulated the suitors and set up the contest of the bow. She and her husband will not need anyone else, not even Athena, to settle their business. However we understand her motivation, we admire the Penelope we find here, who has worked in her own way to bring events to this climax, for her courage, determination, and shrewdness—all qualities we also find in her husband. When the business of disguising what has happened is complete and Odysseus himself has been bathed by Eurynome and made beautiful by Athena, the final negotiations can begin.

Now Odysseus, for the first time, begins to show impatience. His wife is strange, hard, still holding back. Well then, he says with a trace of petulance, let the nurse make my bed, I'll sleep alone! The Greek word that we translate as "strange," *daimoniê*, is potent here. An adjective derived from the noun *daimôn*, "supernatural being," it carries the resonance of the unbridgeable gulf between mortal and immortal in Greek literature, religion, and myth.[24] Mortals can never understand the existence or intentions of the gods, and for one human to call another *daimonios* is to confer on the other an inscrutability well beyond eccentricity. Rather, the word marks an elemental estrangement.

Penelope echoes the beggar, calling him *daimoni(e)*. Her words, of course, carry a further level of significance for us insofar as the man before her is the creation of Athena. She then achieves what no other woman has been able to do since Helen at Troy. Using the ruse of the movable bed, she makes Odysseus lose his self-control and thereby reveal himself when it suits another, not himself, for him to do so (23.177–204). She has tricked the trickster, unmasked the stranger. From this position of strength, she relents, embracing her husband. Not surprisingly, she invokes Helen when explaining herself (23.218–24):

> Argive Helen, born of Zeus, would never
> have mingled in love with a stranger had she
> known that the warlike sons of the Achaeans
> would fight to bring her home again. No,
> some god forced her to act shamefully; not
> before did she conceive in her heart
> the painful blind folly, which brought
> anguish to her and to us as well.

This Penelope is wide awake and ready to answer for herself. Some god brought pain, but they need not prolong the suffering any longer.

HOMOPHROSYNE

It is often said that the last six books of the poem show the operation of *homophrosyne*, "like- mindedness," between Odysseus and Penelope.[25] We can locate the like-mindedness of the royal couple in the context of the alternating perspectives we have been tracing. Penelope, like Odysseus, shows us two different attitudes toward the nature of human life. As the faithful, obedient wife waiting for the return of her husband, she reflects the perspective of the *nostos* plot. Her weaving and unweaving of the shroud, a deception worthy of her devious husband (19.137), can, as I have said, be seen as an attempt to hold back time. This stalling serves the magical *nostos* plot, which also denies the passage of time. On another level, her denial of time is consistent with grieving, a refusal to acknowledge the ongoing rhythms of life: if she cannot be with Odysseus, she might as well be dead. The same impulse is present in her wish, expressed twice (18.201–5; 20.61–65), to have Artemis kill her and in her reluctance to wake up in book 23 (17).

Penelope's reawakening, which begins with the upsetting desire to show herself before the suitors, complicates our understanding of her, as we have seen. Odysseus, she tells us, has told her to move on with her life when Telemachus begins to have a beard. Critics have devised ingenious interpretations of her suggestive dream of the geese and subsequent decision to hold the contest of the bow in an attempt to make her state of mind consistent with the obedient wife of the *nostos* plot. But we might just as well see these acts as a reflection of the trickster in her, setting the stage for centrifugal motion, out of the house in Ithaka, into a new life. This woman, fully alive and entirely capable of manipulating Odysseus with the ruse of the bed, fits uneasily into the static bliss that Athena envisions for her favorite. Her self-sufficiency is that of the trickster, not Athena's puppet; she is *daimonios* to her husband because she reflects back to him his characteristic self-possession and reluctance to reveal herself.

From this perspective, Penelope's invocation of Helen in book 23 is, as we have said, especially suggestive. Her comparison can, of course, be seen as simply a reflection of the fact that she might have been deceived by another man who claimed to be Odysseus, and thus committed adultery like her Spartan counterpart, however innocently. But the parallels between her situation and that of Helen go further than that. Both, as has been often noted, are weavers; both offer a bath to Odysseus when the latter is in disguise; and both succeed in getting him to reveal his identity.[26] With this triumph Penelope transgresses the bounds of the *nostos* plot, revealing the world beyond the magical kingdom of the returning hero. There wives may have impulses that threaten the tight control of the king over his household.

Athena steps in again, stopping time to allow the reunited lovers to enjoy the moment. But the centrifugal Odysseus sneaks back even here, breaking off the embrace to tell Penelope that he will have to go roving again, to follow the instructions given him by Tiresias. For now, however, he wants to go to bed. Overjoyed as she is, Penelope—as if in response to her husband's attempt to keep the door open for further travel—retains some leverage for just a little longer. They can certainly go to bed, but first he must tell her what exactly the prophecy is. Her ploy preserves the wary mood of their earlier standoff: *Daimoniê*, he says, why do you want to force me to tell more secrets? He then reveals the details, to which she replies, "If the gods will bring a happier old age, perhaps there's some hope of our escaping evil after all" (23.286–87).

The royal couple finally go to bed and after lovemaking tell each other their stories. The narratives are brief—especially that of Penelope—and in the third person, providing nothing new for us. The reports on both sides are, in fact, somewhat elliptical. Odysseus tells only of his trials, not of his pleasures; Penelope recalls her struggles with the suitors but gives no hint that she might have enjoyed their attention.[27] The queen's editing is the last evidence we will see of her centrifugal independence.

After letting her favorite catch up on his sleep, Athena intervenes again to bring on the dawn. She has other plans for him (23.344–48). Odysseus arises with the future on his mind. He tells Penelope that, happy as he is to be reunited with her, he must now be off. He will, he assures her, replenish the livestock by raiding but must now go to see his father. She, meanwhile, must stay in the bedroom, see no one, speak to no one. This is the final direct glimpse we get of Penelope, who is returned to the role of passive wife, waiting for her husband.

The "like-mindedness" of Odysseus and Penelope is usually understood in the context of the *nostos* plot.[28] That is, though the queen shows evidence of a wiliness and self-possession that mirrors her husband's, it is all in the service of restoring the magic kingdom in Ithaka. I have suggested that we expand this perspective to include the wider world beyond the return plot. That is, the *homophrosyne* is not just that of the faithful king and queen but also of the deceitful trickster and the resourceful, independent weaver. The awakening of Penelope and her subsequent machinations can be seen, like the trickery of her husband, as either centripetal or centrifugal. To Odysseus' deceptions and self-concealment, Penelope responds with active manipulation of both people (including Odysseus) and events.[29]

FINALE: BOOK 24

Book 24 is almost entirely presented from the point of view of the return plot. First, the suitors are seen making their dismal way to Hades, where they meet heroes more illustrious than they. From Achilles we hear again of the ignominious death of Agamemnon, who then recounts at length the funeral of Achilles, then hails his old friend Amphimedon, one of the dead suitors. The latter then recalls the events in Ithaka that led to the death of the suitors: Penelope's ruse, the infiltration of the palace by Odysseus, the abuse of the beggar, his triumph in the contest of the bow, and his final bloody vengeance. The story prompts a fresh burst of admiration from Agamemnon for Odysseus and Penelope, whose virtues allowed them to escape the bitter fate that awaited him upon his return (24.1–202).

These lines have a clear function in the architecture of the *nostos* plot. We see the suitors, whose moral failings have been offered as a justification for their slaughter, properly delivered to their allotted fates. To clinch the argument, Achilles and Agamemnon are brought on as heroic foils, the former's *kleos* certified by his lavish funeral, the latter's undeserved suffering recalled again to highlight Odysseus' near miss. It can all be explained, and it all seems slightly mechanical. Unlike Odysseus' *katabasis*, in which the contrast between the hero's continuing struggle for life and the melancholy finality of the existence of the dead lent energy to the lifeless scenes, this episode is unrelievedly dreary and hopeless. The tone here is hard: heroes who win are justly celebrated, and the losers can expect at best to be famous, like Agamemnon, as the victims of treachery. With perhaps the exception of Amphinomos, who does not appear in this episode, we have not been encouraged to think of the suitors as complex human beings. They exist to be foils and then to be killed. In the gloomy finality of Hades, they are of even less interest.

Now comes the reunion between Odysseus and Laertes, which we have discussed, and then the final showdown with the families of the suitors. The theme of this conclusion is restoration. Odysseus is finally to reinhabit his rightful status, Laertes will return to the palace, all will be well. Athena is busy now, as we expect. She makes Laertes broader and taller, to mirror the earlier transformation of Odysseus, in both cases producing a younger version, turning back time. Before the last standoff, she goes to Zeus to ask whether he plans to prolong the fighting or bring peace. His reply echoes their conversation before Odysseus is freed from Calypso (24.478–86):

> My child, why keep questioning me about these things?
> This is your plan, is it not, to have Odysseus come home
> and pay those suitors back? Do whatever you wish.
> But I will tell you how it should be. Since Odysseus has
> repaid the suitors, let both sides strike binding oaths,
> that he should rule all his life, and we will make them
> forget the bloody slaughter of their brothers and sons.
> Let them love each other as before; let peace and wealth
> be present everywhere.

True to the perspective of the return plot, the reign of Odysseus is to be ensured by canceling out the ravages of time and circumstance. Athena lets the battle go a little longer, arriving herself in the guise of Medon. Laertes gets to kill one man, the luckless Eupeithes, before Athena screams and stops everyone but Odysseus in their tracks. He refuses to hold back until the goddess commands him directly, and then finally relents.

The poem ends abruptly, as we have said and many others have observed. But beyond that structural problem lies another, which may help to account for the curiously flat conclusion to such an otherwise exciting story: nowhere in book 24 do we see action proceeding from the genuine collision of character and circumstance. Everyone's role has been determined by its function within the architecture of the return plot, and, perhaps with the sole exception of the reunion of Odysseus and Laertes, everyone follows the script. As he does elsewhere in the narrative, the poet seems to point insistently at the divine machinery of the *nostos* plot as if to ensure that we attend to the implications of his determinedly focused perspective. Having followed the stranger and the trickster through the poem, we are in a better position now to understand these implications. It is precisely the subversive elements in the king and queen that we miss as the story comes to a close because it is in their world that humans interact and touch one another amid the necessities of time. Once the beggar leaves the stage for good, once the shadow of Helen passes away, Odysseus and Penelope have lost their connection to the fragile existence of mortals and must negotiate without the liberating compassion that exists only there.

In the conclusion to chapter 2, we identified two visions of human life that seem to coexist in the *Odyssey*. In the clash between those perspectives, we began to locate the source of the difficulties that many have seen in the end of the poem. Specifically, the Odysseus who returns to Ithaka does not feel like someone who can remain there, even though he has in some ways been defined by his position within the royal family. Likewise, there is no room in the restored kingdom for a Penelope who would stray, even in her dreams. In subsequent chapters, we have been developing various paradigms through which we can understand further the subversive aspects of Odysseus' character. We have traced their implications for the character of Penelope in particular and also for the overall view of human life that the *Odyssey* offers. We may be content to say that the tensions in the character of the principals add spice and therefore interest to the story and leave it at that. But if we want to pursue the question of why the poem has maintained such a strong hold on the imaginations of readers across the millennia, we will need to go further.

The *Odyssey* is articulated throughout by a recurring cycle of movement and stasis, often realized more specifically as capture and release. Telemachus is stalled in Ithaka, and Athena must release him to grow. Odysseus is trapped by Calypso, and Hermes effects his release. Nausicaa would hold the hero in marriage, but he talks his way to freedom and a ride back to Ithaka. The pattern continues in the adventures, as forces of all kinds hold back Odysseus or threaten to do so: the Cicones, Lotus Eaters, Polyphemus, Circe, Hades, perhaps Antikleia, and Poseidon. Athena orchestrates many of these escapes, pushing her favorite toward the restoration she wants for him. But alongside that level of motivation is another, the extraordinary intelligence, wiliness, and determination of the hero himself. These latter qualities are associated in the crucial Calypso episode with Odysseus' existential self-creation through action, contrasted strongly there with the forces of stasis and oblivion represented by the nymph's offer.

These patterns of action are firmly established in the first half of the poem, and so we look for them when the hero finally arrives in Ithaka. The trouble is, however, that the blissful state toward which Odysseus strives exhibits qualities that we cannot help but see as analogous to the stasis that is so threatening to the hero elsewhere. And the loyal wife who waits at the center of his existence, at least as the return plot constructs it, resembles in troubling ways the dangerous detaining women who have clung to Odysseus throughout his journey. To put it another way, the hero's triumphant restoration looks disturbingly like a capture; the world he would live in as Athena's favorite is closed off from much of human experience, another island of oblivion. As he has throughout the poem, so here we expect the hero to escape the attempted capture. But he cannot in this instance expect help from Athena, it would appear, since she has presided over the restoration of the closed world. Odysseus is on his own this time. This is where the paradigms of the stranger and the trickster become crucial. Both offer escape through an alternate universe from that of the return plot.

At the same time, the approach of Odysseus seems to stir in Penelope a new assertiveness. Ironically, the closer he gets to clinching his prize the more dangerously active that prize becomes; as the trickster in him surfaces, her own wiliness and self-sufficiency come forward; he descends to shriveled ugliness, she emerges from grief to lure the suitors. This dance is part of the cliffhanger aspect of the story's penultimate scenes but also continues the dual perspective that has informed the poem from its beginning.

To be the Odysseus of the *nostos* plot, the hero must be defined by the parameters of its magical venue, outside of time and change. His existence is defined by status, as king, husband, father, son. He is worthy because he is different from other men, more intelligent, more determined, stronger: *kleos* separates. There is, in the context of the poem's structure, a trap of fame that awaits Odysseus in Ithaka. Likewise, Penelope's quiescence in the beginning of the poem and in its final scenes is the price of her participation in the restoration. Swept along by the excitement and wish fulfillment in the story of the king's return, we would not be thinking about this aspect of the settlement in books 18–24 if the poet had not shown us other ways to understand Odysseus' existence. On Scheria, in the cave of the Cyclops, on the island of Circe we see the freedom in being nobody. To be known immediately as Odysseus to Nausicaa, the monster, or the witch would have put the hero in various kinds of potent binds. Likewise, the isolation that comes with fame is thrown into relief by the rich encounters in the hut of the swineherd. The beggar is free to form bonds of friendship with whomever he pleases; Odysseus would be welcomed but also walled off from intimacy.

Once inside the palace walls, the beggar continues to profit from anonymity. As in the Cyclops' cave, so here Odysseus is free to size up the adversary and make plans. But beyond that, we see that while he remains nobody Odysseus is also free of the zero-sum imperatives of Athena's revenge calculus. He can make contact with Amphinomos and respond to the suitor as a person, attempting to modulate his own actions according to a more humane and subtle view of human motivation than can the triumphant avenger who slaughters everyone in book 22.

This latter aspect of the beggar brings us back into contact with the trickster, a figure who can always profit from anonymity. Because he crosses boundaries, the trickster combats the violence that can result from the desire for purity. The beggar has been on the margins of life and is not defined by his presence within a magic circle. Nor does he feel compelled to enforce the sanctity of the circle. The absolutist nature of Athena's perspective on the suitors' acts is founded on a clearly demarcated boundary between right and wrong action. Her hero must keep the dirt of the suitors outside the restored world of the royal palace. The beggar as trickster tries to keep the circle porous, to let Amphinomos enter and then exit, but Athena cannot allow it.

We might say that while the stranger can slip the trap of fame, the trickster offers escape from the trap of stasis. The settlement that the hero of the revenge plot and his divine companion would impose implies a negation of the passage of time, a passage that is itself a kind of motion. The centripetal drive of the hero in this perspective aims to finish at a still point, represented in the poem by the olive tree in the middle of the palace. To lie in the bed is to have reached perfection, the fulfillment of all desire—both the desire of the returning king and husband and our own desire to see the story end happily. Like all such worlds, this one is alluring but finally restricting, even suffocating. The centrifugal hero is no sooner in postcoital ease than he begins to talk of motion, journeys to be taken. Telemachus, meanwhile, has grown up, and Laertes has grown old. Athena keeps the timeless world in place for a little longer in book 24 by making Laertes younger, by preserving the three-generation hierarchy in the final abortive showdown. But even in the midst of this perfect moment, time's passing is noted. Odysseus gives Telemachus a pep talk: when he's had some experience of fighting (when he's a real man), he'll learn not to disgrace his lineage. Telemachus retorts with some sharpness (24.511–12):

> You will see, father dear, if you wish to, that I
> will not, as you say, disgrace your line with this heart!

The son has already grown up and is impatient living within the narrow confines of this heroic dream.

By crossing and recrossing boundaries, the trickster disenchants the world included within them. In place of the narrow perfection of purity, he can point the way to a richer plenitude, a wider world unavailable to those who have hypnotized themselves into believing that the world is contained within the magic circle. The poet of the *Odyssey* tells more than one story about the world in his poem. He gives us the thrilling return of the hero articulated within a satisfyingly simple milieu of heroes and villains, full of suspense and miraculous close calls. But the *Odyssey* would never have survived to enchant us if that were all there was to the story. Behind the taut and focused narrative of Odysseus' magical triumph lies a different and richer world filled with flawed mortals working the dirt, growing old and gentle. Homer implies that we need both kinds of worlds and that we cannot be defined adequately by a narrow hierarchy of worth. We began with the question, who is Odysseus? The *Odyssey* seems to say, paradoxically, that we must continue to ask this about him and about ourselves but that we must also beware of thinking that we have found the answer.

EPILOGUE

WOR(L)DS

I called you naughty boy because I do not like that other world.
Please tell me what is the real meaning of that word?

James Joyce, *Ulysses*

To make one's way in the *Odyssey* requires a good story. Escaping a monster's cave, angling for a boat ride, earning a meal all depend on creating a world with words. Not surprisingly, the best storyteller in the poem is Odysseus, but many other narrators pass before us: Phemius, "Mentes," Nestor, Menelaus, Helen, Demodocus, Eumaeus, Theoclymenus, Penelope. Some tell stories about themselves, some about others. Some of their work is presented by the poet of the *Odyssey* as "true," some "false," but the stream of stories is constant. We might say that the most characteristic act in the poem is creative storytelling.

We also discover early on another layer of narration inside the frame of the poem but once removed from the stories the other characters tell. Athena has her own tale, which she must have told at least to Zeus, about how Odysseus would return home and vanquish the suitors.[1] She comes to complain in book 5 because the happy ending she has envisioned is imperiled by Calypso. Her father is surprised at her anxiety: hasn't she arranged all this beforehand? Make it happen! The poem ends with Zeus repeating his injunctions in the same words and Athena promptly dis-

121

posing of events (6.22–24; 24.478–80). And so we learn that however the mortal characters in the story may be shown to experience their lives, from the perspective of Olympus, they are all part of a prearranged game. There is nothing unusual about this dual perspective for the characters or for us as readers. Greek literature is founded on ironies generated by the divide between divine and human existence. And yet, the poet of the *Odyssey* seems especially intent on emphasizing that the return plot is, literally, artificial, that it implies a fictive world that is neither identical to nor coextensive with "the *Odyssey*."

We see the goddess as artist come to prominence—working in these cases in a different artistic medium—at moments when her creation is under particularly strong pressure to be alluring, before Nausicaa on the beach and before Penelope after the slaughter of the suitors (6.229–35; 23.156–62). The simile is explicit:

> As when some skilled man, whom Hephaestus and Athena
> taught every technique, pours gold over silver,
> and brings to perfection his graceful art,
> so she poured grace over his head and shoulders.

The *Odyssey* is, as we have said, unusually self-conscious about itself as artifice. At the center of all its creativity is the return plot itself and within that artifice another creation, the returning hero, triumphant over all that would block the proper ending for his story.

Next comes the story told by the poet of the *Odyssey*, structurally sophisticated, complex in its presentation of multiple fictive worlds. The return story of Athena is embedded in this layer of narration along with other tales, variously told, some of which belong to a different world than that which the goddess requires for her story. Which brings us finally to the last layer of storytellers, all of us who have heard or read the poem in the last three millennia. We tend to think of ourselves, when reading, as passively receiving the text. But, as theories of "reader-response" would argue, every reader of a text participates in the creation of the narrative.[2] If the storyteller is Virgil or James Joyce, the retelling can become itself a new work of art. But all acts of interpretation can be understood for our purposes here as a retelling.

By focusing on the centrifugal aspects of Odysseus' character, I have been arguing for a different relationship among the three outermost lay-ers of storytelling than has been customary among readers (or perhaps I should say narrators) of the *Odyssey*. I have suggested that by detaching ourselves from the imperatives of Athena's story we open ourselves more fully to a wider perspective, one that implies quite a different world, structured by an alternate set of assumptions about human life and death. Such a perspective does not challenge what the poet presents as true or false but simply acknowledges other stories as part of the full representation of human life that the poem offers. By including the "false" personae, we gain access to a different hero. In place of the relentlessly focused, ruthlessly efficient avenger, we find a man with wider sympathies, open to experiences the disguised king would avoid, to people he can only experience as instruments. The trickster subverts rigid hierarchical structures and opens them up to let fresh air blow through. Such a man is *polytropos* in ways that Athena's favorite cannot be. Penelope, too, becomes more vivid in the sum of her personae as not only dutiful wife but also resourceful, independent woman, alert to the present, looking to the future, not trapped in grief over what has passed.

The world around this traveler opens up with him. The unremitting urgency, so crucial to the return plot, eases in the hut of Eumaeus, on the island of Circe. Stratified social arrangements, reflecting a scale of values determined by the heroic will to power, are balanced by a more compassionate, interdependent set of relationships. A monocular monster can be seen not simply as an obstacle to the hero's glory, to be conquered with no second thoughts, but also as the lonely, grotesque shepherd finding comfort in the mute witness of his ram. The better parts of Amphinomos, whom Athena must condemn along with all the other suitors, could win him a reprieve.

A question remains: does the poem *valorize* the world of the stranger or is it simply a matter of our teasing these meanings out of the text, working against the grain of the poet's vision? Can we say that the *Odyssey*, like the *Iliad*, presents within itself an alternative to the dominant heroic perspective, which finally, as does the meeting of Priam and Achilles in *Iliad* 24, recasts our perspective on how to evaluate a human life? Although no definitive answer could or ought to be given to such a question, my arguments here invite some kind of response. From the perspective we have been pursuing, the question arises inevitably from the poem's insistence on identifying Athena's return plot as divine artifice, as one story being told about Odysseus and his homecoming but not the only story. The exchange between Amphinomos and the beggar points in the same direction by allowing us to see the goddess's remorseless vengeance from a different—if fleeting—vantage point just before the triumphant slaughter. The poet of the *Odyssey* creates the hardest, most unrelenting portrait of masculine heroic will in all of Greek literature. But, as is the case with so many enduring works from the classical world, he delineates his hero against a more complex backdrop, which prompts us to assess his allure more thoughtfully, to pause before giving ourselves over to the world his return demands.

THE USES OF ANONYMITY

Many Americans at the turn of the millennium are entranced by the lure of being known—for anything, by anyone. Our obsession has been abetted by an explosion of technology that has provided myriad new possibilities for self-display. The surge toward notoriety is presently reaching its apogee on the Internet, where the boundaries between public and private have been blurred dramatically. Personal Web pages proliferate by the hundreds (thousands?) every day. Proud parents show pictures of their newborn children, campers share their summer vacations, with anyone who logs on.

Another aspect of contemporary American culture that both finds expression in and is driven by the latest technological revolution is a more malleable sense of self. The proliferation of images, infinitely reproducible in numberless venues, now promotes a weakening of the modernist notion of an inner, core self that reveals itself through outward behavior. The potential for a new kind of contingency has entered our notions of identity. As Kenneth Gergen has recently said of the "postmodern" self, "One's identity is continuously emergent, re-formed, and redirected as one moves through the sea of ever-changing relationships. In the case of 'who am I?' it is a teeming world of provisional possibilities."[3] This new paradigm has not met with universal acceptance, much less approval. Many find the decentered nature of the postmodern self to be threatening, even sinister. Others experience the flexibility implied by provisional identities as exhilarating. Whatever the variety of responses, these two cultural phenomena are mutually reinforcing. The ability to reinvent ourselves answers the yearning for celebrity: if we cannot be famous as one person, we can become another. And if our fame fades, the loss is not so great if there is no core self that must be propped up by notoriety.

The *Odyssey* provides a fruitful perspective on these preoccupations. The heroic obsession with *kleos,* and its consequent horror at the prospect of namelessness, demands celebrity. In this view, to be unknown is the same as being dead. And yet anonymity, as we have seen, also has its uses. To be fixed by the gaze of admiring millions can be, paradoxically, isolating; to be nobody opens doors closed to the famous. The hero, by nature *egregious,* reenters the flock with difficulty. At the same time, no one is better at reinventing himself than Odysseus, who is surely—at least during his return home—the first postmodern hero.

The *Odyssey*'s hero exists in different worlds simultaneously, something the postmodern consciousness can accommodate, even welcome, but in his persona as protagonist of the *nostos* he is driven by goals not consistent with the "continuously emergent, re-formed, and redirected" identity that Gergen describes. On the contrary: to reach home as it is realized at Ithaka is to be motionless, unavailable for re-formation. It is precisely in these alternative perspectives that the poem can help us sort through the implications of our society's present obsessions. Continuous, centrifugal reinvention of oneself precludes reaching home, but with the opposite extreme, reaching the center and closing oneself off in the stability of home, comes paralysis. There must be a center but not one that is founded principally on negation of change: the wandering, nameless trickster must always be able to find a way into the magic circle, to keep a path open for the unexpected. James Joyce, having finally brought his wandering hero back home to lie beside Molly Bloom in the bed at the center of the world, leaves them right where the *Odyssey* recommends:

> At rest relatively to themselves and to each other. In motion being each and both carried westward, forward and rereward respectively, by the proper perpetual motion of the earth through everchanging tracks of neverchanging space. (*Ulysses,* 606)

NOTES

1. Felson (1997), though focusing on Penelope, also analyzes "possible plots," story lines that are raised by the poet and then not pursued (see x–xi), which in turn suggest alternate ways for characters to develop. Peradotto (1990) explores potential variants in the plot and the poem's hero. See especially pages 59–93. Pucci (1987, 13–15) suggests two contrasting readings of the *Odyssey* organized around the question of whether or not Odysseus changes in the course of his journey. My reading is also contiguous with studies of the poem by Katz (1991), who focuses on the element of "indeterminacy" in the character of Penelope, an openness that is achieved within the text by a form of intetextuality, and Doherty (1995), who discusses the relationship between "open" and "closed" readings of the *Odyssey*. Perhaps most important for my thesis is the succinct definition by Murnaghan (1987, 178) of the "two contrasting visions" that the *Odyssey* holds in suspense. This excellent book, which I believe has not yet received the recognition it deserves, has been seminal in many ways for my own work. See also Gregory (1996, 17–19). Buchan (2004) reached me after I had completed the writing of this book. I am interested to see that, though his approach is quite different from mine, he has been drawn to many of the same qualities in the poem that I address here. In particular, his chapters 6 and 7 explore, working from Peradotto's poststructuralist paradigm and the ideas of Lacan and Žižek, the implications of other personae for Odysseus. I am sorry to have missed the chance to acknowledge more fully the fascinating reading of the poem that Buchan offers.

2. Peradotto (1990, 53–58).

3. See Stanford (1963, 81–89); Clarke (1981).

4. Hyde (1998, 171–99).

CHAPTER ONE

1. See Stanford (1963); Clarke (1981).

2. Pucci (1987) argues for a complex intertextuality between the two Homeric poems, asserting not only that many passages in the *Odyssey* can be read against the background of specific passages from the *Iliad* but also vice versa.

3. See Murnaghan (1987, 84).

4. The question of succession in the house of Odysseus is vexed. It is not at all clear why Telemachus ought not be the presumptive king of Ithaka in the event of his father's death (e.g, 1.387) or why Laertes is not the king in his son's absence. M. Finley (1978, 84–85) notes these difficulties and assumes that the proper succession must be patrilineal. More recently Finkelberg (1991) makes a compelling argument for a system of kingship by marriage existing in a society that was politically controlled by men.

5. On *polytropos*, see Nagy (1990, 18–35); Murnaghan (1987, 10); Pucci (1987, 16–17, 127–28, 149, 150); Murnaghan (1995); Clay (1983, 30–31); Hyde (1998, 51–54); Marquardt (1985).

6. On Athena's role as protectress of Odysseus, see Stanford (1963, 25–42); for Athena as orchestrator of the return plot, see Reinhardt (1960, 45) and Felson (1997, 5), who sees the "opposing actions" of Athena and Poseidon as constituting the *Odyssey* plot. Pucci (1987, 19–22) stresses the role of Athena.

7. On the theme of hospitality in the *Odyssey*, see Reece (1993); Edwards (1975); Lateiner (1993); Pedrick (1988).

8. Wohl (1993, 24).

9. On this scene, see Pucci (1987, 195–208).

10. The meaning of this speech for the *Odyssey*'s portrayal of divine justice has been much discussed. See, for example, Clay (1983, 213–39); Rutherford (1986, 148); Friedrich (1987); Nagler (1990); Segal (1992).

11. On the family of Agamemnon as paradigmatic for the *Odyssey*, see further Olson (1990) with bibliography.

12. See note 10.

13. On Telemachus and the Telemachia, see Calhoun (1934); Clarke (1963); Rose (1967); Murnaghan (1987, 34–37, 159–66); Felson (1997, 67–91).

14. See Felson (1997, 95–96) on a possible alternate trajectory for Telemachus, following Aegisthus.

15. On the contest of the bow, see Clay (1983, 89–96).

16. See Murnaghan (1987, 160).

17. On the stories of Menelaus and Agamemnon as vehicles for creating irony and suspense, see Olson (1989); Felson (1997, 97–99).

18. Murnaghan (1987, 8–9) notes the connection between Odysseus' endurance in the *Odyssey* and his use of disguise; see also Pucci (1987, 76–79).

19. For the parallels between Menelaus and Odysseus, see Anderson (1958).

20. Felson (1997, 99).

21. I remember hearing, when I was a little boy after World War II, stories about Japanese soldiers who had wandered out of the jungle unaware that the

war was over. One imagines a disjunction in these men between their understanding of the world and what they found that is analogous to the situation of Odysseus, who is still fighting while his comrades have moved on to another kind of existence.

22. For Telemachus' journeys as part of a pattern of doubling with Odysseus, see Fenik (1974, 26ff.).

23. See note 18.

24. Murnaghan (1987, 160).

25. On this passage, see Pucci (1987, 20–21).

26. On the suitors as blameworthy, see Levy (1963); Dimock (1970); Murnaghan (1987, 77); Pucci (1987, 68 n.14); Katz (1991, 172).

27. For the suitors as immature but also at times sympathetic, see Felson (1997, 109–23).

28. See Edwards (1987, 49).

29. For a sensitive discussion of Calypso's island as a reflection of her divinity, see Austin (1975, 149–52).

30. On singing and narration in the *Odyssey*, see Mackie (1997); Scodel (1998).

31. Austin (1975, 142–43).

32. On spinning, weaving, and singing, see Pantelia (1993); Snyder (1981); Bergren (1983).

33. See Van Nortwick (1980).

34. See Austin (1975, 138–39).

35. See Peradotto (1990, 102–3); Felson (1997, 44–46).

36. Scully (1987, 415–16).

37. See Austin (1975, 151).

38. Ibid., 138–39.

39. See Russo (1966) for the implications of such passages for our understanding of Homeric formulaic style.

40. See Nagy (1979, 298–300, 311) on the relationship between carpentry and poetics in the Indo-European tradition.

41. See Carson (1990, 42); Austin (1975, 139).

42. See Nagler (1974, 64–76).

43. See Van Nortwick (1979, 270–71).

44. On *kaluptô* and Calypso, see Peradotto (1990, 102–6).

45. See, on this simile, Foley (1978).

CHAPTER TWO

1. See Austin (1975, 138–41) for a good discussion of the threat of oblivion, especially as it relates to memory.

2. For the existential implications of naming, see Peradotto (1990, 92–170); Austin (1972); Webber (1989, 12–13). See also Whitman (1958, 300–301) on naming and identity.

3. For example, see Bradley (1976, 144); Tracy (1990, 61–62, 74).

4. See Whitman (1958, 299).

5. On the stories in 9–12 as manipulative, see Most (1989); Felson (1997, 99–100); Hyde (1998, 68).

6. One of the anonymous readers at the University of Michigan Press reminds me that the Homeric narrator does confirm some details of the stories, for example, the Cattle of the Sun at 1.7–9 and Circe at 8.447–48. See Most (1989, 19).

7. Tracy (1990, 57) suggests that by juxtaposing Odysseus' wanderings to his return to Ithaka Homer makes these stories exceptionally vivid; Most (1989, 17) sees the placement of the *apologoi* as a device to avoid a lengthy digression in book 23.

8. The best work on Homeric repetition as a device for building meaning remains Fenik (1974).

9. On Nausicaa, see Austin (1975, 193–94, 202–3); Gross (1976); Van Nortwick (1979).

10. On women as flowing across boundaries, see Carson (1990).

11. See Felson (1997, 47).

12. On Polyphemus' orderliness, see Austin (1975, 143–44).

13. For the role of singing, see Mackie (1997); Wohl (1993, 23, 34). On "voice," see Nagler (1977).

14. On the Sirens, see Pucci (1979); Scodel (1998, 188–99).

15. For the Phaeacians as threatening, see Rose (1969).

16. See Austin (1975, 153–62).

17. For the function of the Phaeacian episode in the return of Odysseus to himself, see Segal (1962).

18. Felson (1997, 49).

19. Murnaghan (1987, 77).

20. Austin (1975, 227).

21. Dimock (1956); see also note 2.

22. See Van Nortwick (1992, 79–88).

23. Stanford (1958, 2:409–10) summarizes the objections of scholiasts; for a defense of *Odyssey* 24, see Wender (1978).

24. See Heubeck in Russo, Fernandez-Galiano, and Heubeck (1992, 342–45).

25. On the cruelty of Odysseus, see Page (1955, 111–12); and, contra, J. Finley (1978, 224–33).

26. Shaeffer (1949).

27. See Pantelia (1993, 497); Felson (1997, 19–20, 26–28).

28. See Amory (1963, 101).

29. Van Nortwick (1979, 273–76).

30. See Felson (1997, 128).

31. Virgil picks up this aspect of Athena's intervention at *Aeneid* 1.586–93 where Venus presents her son to Dido. See Van Nortwick (1992, 102).

32. Murnaghan (1987, 178).

33. On this aspect of Odysseus' characterization, see Whitman (1958, 285–309); Segal (1962); Pucci (1987, 15).

34. See note 10.

35. For Penelope's reticence as evidence of her "indignation," see Roisman (1987).

36. Penelope's comparison of herself to Helen has generated considerable controversy. See, for example, Morgan (1991); Frederiksmeyer (1997).

37. Van Nortwick (1992, 86–88).

38. Kermode (1979, 78–79).

CHAPTER THREE

1. The best discussion of "the stranger" as a repeated motif in the poem is Fenik (1974, 5–60). See also Murnaghan (1987); Stewart (1976); Pucci (1987, 83–89).

2. See Beye (1987, 156).

3. For the ninth century BCE as background, see M. Finley (1978). Whitman (1958, 308) suggests aspects of the poem that reflect the seventh century. For the latter view, see also van Wees (2002).

4. For Nausicaa and Arete as paradigms for Penelope, see Van Nortwick (1979).

5. For this metaphor in the poem, see Lateiner (1992, 150).

6. See Felson (1997, 173–74 n.15).

7. On the question of whether the punishment is carried out, see Peradotto (1990, 77–82).

8. On the Phaeacians as liminal, see Segal (1962).

9. For an exhaustive review of the folktale background, see Glenn (1971). See also Page (1955, 1–20); Schein (1970); Mondi (1983).

10. On Polyphemus' order, see Austin (1975, 143–49).

11. For Polyphemus as sympathetic, see Newton (1983).

12. See Dimock (1956).

13. On Circe and Calypso, see Austin (1975, 152–53), who also suggests parallels between Circe and Polyphemus. See also Nagler (1977); Scully (1987, 406–8); Wohl (1993, 23–27).

14. Cf. *Odyssey* 6.18–19, 21.45–46, 22.201; Homeric *Hymn to Aphrodite* 60, 236.

15. It is usually assumed that Odysseus has no help from Athena during his adventures. Clay (1983) makes the argument that the goddess is absent because she is angry at Odysseus. Sometimes Odysseus knows things about the gods that ought to be unavailable to him, so we might assume that he would know if Athena helped him with Circe as she did with Calypso.

16. See, for example, the Homeric *Hymn to Aphrodite* 177–90.

17. For the "consolation motif" in Greek literature, see Nagler (1974, 174–77).

18. Tracy (1990) sees Circe as a serious threat to Odysseus.

19. See Van Nortwick (1992, 180–81).

20. Ibid., 27–28, 86–88.

21. The earliest mention of the encounter with snakes seems to be in Hesiod, fr. 275, and the earliest full account in Apollodorus 3.6.7. See also *Metamorphoses* 3.314–36.

22. See Van Nortwick (1998, 48–50).

23. Bassi (1999, 420–21).

24. Ibid., 419; see also Wohl (1993, 36–37).

25. Austin (1975, 137).

26. Kermode (1979, 54).

CHAPTER FOUR

1. See, for example, Kirk (1962, 358).

2. See Murnaghan (1997, 97).

3. On the exchange between Athena and Odysseus, see Stanford (1963, 30–36); Clay (1983, 186–212); Pucci (1987, 83–89).

4. Reece (1993) makes the case for an alternative story of Odysseus's return, which had him landing in Crete. This is intriguing, and entirely possible, I suppose, but given the centrality of lying in the poem, references to Crete do not need explanation.

5. See, for example, Stanford (1963, 31–34).

6. See Austin (1975, 165–68); Edwards (1993, 60).

7. See Hölscher (1939, 66); Fenik (1974, 23–24, 155–58).

8. See Kearns (1982); Burnett (1970, 24–25 n.8).

9. See Fenik (1974, 233–44).

10. Edwards (1993) provides a full and convincing description of the ethical differences that characterize the countryside as compared to the city in the *Odyssey*. His distinctions parallel mine here. See especially pages 27, 49, 63, 69, and 76. See also Rose (1992, 92–140) on the countryside as the negation of traditional heroic values. For Eumaeus, see Thalmann (1998, 84–100). Aimless wandering is also one characteristic of the trickster; see Hyde (1998, 96).

11. See Mackie (1997, 87); Thalmann (1984, 162).

12. For Telemachus, see Fenik (1974, 23–60); for Menelaus, see Anderson (1958).

13. On the doubling, see Fenik (1974, 166).

14. On Theoclymenus, see further ibid., 233–44.

15. Austin (1975, 165).

16. On Phemius and Demodocus, see further Pucci (1987, 195–235).

17. On the parallels between the "true" and "false" tales, see Beye (1987, 46–47); Doherty (2002). See also Hyde (1998, 66–67).

18. For fluid identity as characteristic of the trickster, see Hyde (1998, 54).

19. For a somewhat different understanding of these distinctions, see Scodel (1998, 172–73).

CHAPTER FIVE

1. On this scene, see Clay (1983, 56–69); Peradotto (1990, 120–42).

2. See Hölscher (1989) for the folktale background.

3. See Dimock (1956); Dimock (1989, 246–63); Peradotto (1990, 94–142).

4. Hyde (1998).

5. On Hermes as trickster, see Brown (1947); Hyde (1998, 203–25).

6. See Hyde (1998, 285–86).

7. Ibid., 171–99; see further, on "dirt," Carson (1990).

8. Hyde (1998, 198).

9. Wohl (1993, 22).

10. For the trickster and lying, see Hyde (1998, 55–80).

11. Ibid., 65.

12. Ibid., 64–65.

13. Ibid., 335–43.

14. See further Van Nortwick (1992, 86–87).

15. See Nagler (1974, 174–96).

16. Cf. *Iliad* 24.24.

17. See, most recently, Russo (1997).

18. See chapter 4, 78–79.

19. See Felson (1997, 131–32); Martin (1989, 146–205).

20. Hyde (1998, 218).

21. Ibid., 209.

22. Ibid., 213. See also Hermes' precocious and efficacious speeches at Homeric *Hymn to Hermes* 261–77 and 268–86.

23. See Austin (1972).

CHAPTER SIX

1. See Felson (1997, 111–13); Wohl (1993, 24).

2. For the detaining woman and memory, see Austin (1975, 139–40).

3. See Murnaghan (1987, 128ff); (1995, 70ff.).

4. On Amphinomos, see Felson (1997, 120–21).

5. See Pucci (1987, 222) for a different but analogous distinction between Odysseus as "listener" and "heroic doer."

6. Quoted in Hyde (1998, 293).

7. See Wohl (1993, 24).

8. Ibid., 22.

9. Felson (1997, 84–86) sees Telemachus, when he brings Odysseus home, as "fathering" Odysseus.

10. The bibliography on Penelope, especially for the last twenty years or so, is extensive. Felson (1997) has an excellent bibliography. See also Murnaghan (1987); Katz (1991).

11. On this scene, see Van Nortwick (1979), on which the interpretation here is based, with bibliography. Now see also Levine (1983); Emlyn-Jones (1984); Byre (1988); Wohl (1993, 40–41); Felson (1997, 128–29).

12. On this phrase, see Levine (1983).

13. On this point, however, see Van Nortwick (1979, 273); Wohl (1993, 10–11).

14. Olson (1990); Felson (1997, 93–94).

15. See Pucci (1987, 84–85).

16. Van Nortwick (1979, 272 n. 13).

17. Ibid., 275–76.

18. Amory (1963, 101).

19. Nagler (1974, 176–77); Van Nortwick (1992, 26–28, 67–69).

20. On the shroud, see the thorough analysis of Lowenstam (2000), who suggests that the ambivalence of weaving and unweaving reflects Penelope's shifting attitude toward Odysseus' return.

21. On the ambiguity in Penelope's character, see Murnaghan (1986).

22. On the relationship between Telemachus and his mother, see Wohl (1993, 38–40); Felson (1997, 21–22, 52–53, 82–83).

23. See further Pucci (1987, 89–94).

24. The adjective marks an analogously strained exchange between Hector and Andromache in *Iliad* 6; see Van Nortwick (2001, 225–30).

25. See, for example, Austin (1975, 202–38); Russo (1982).

26. For Helen as a possible paradigm for Penelope, see Wohl (1993, 33–36, 44).

27. Felson (1997, 41).

28. But see Wohl (1993, 44).

29. The Penelope I envision here is in the spirit of the Penelope of Winkler (1990, 129–61), who took me to task for excessive psychologizing (155) in Van Nortwick (1979). I still find his use of modern Greek material problematic but now see the implications of my own findings differently than I did earlier.

EPILOGUE

1. Pucci (1987) calls attention to Athena's "split role as a secret persuader and mover of characters and as an openly divine presence for us. . . . In her split role Athena belongs simultaneously to the world dialogue of the characters and to the world dialogue of the narrator- reader and fulfills the specific narrative function of accounting for both worlds. While she still belongs to the world of the serious epic orthodoxy, she also belongs to the world of the specific fiction her role helps to create" (115). Pucci is not interested in quite the same aspects of Athena's storytelling as I am here, but his formulation of her mediating function is consistent with my own.

2. Felson (1997) and Doherty (1995) each address the role of audiences in creating meaning.

3. Gergen (1991, 139).

REFERENCE LIST

Amory, A. 1963. The Reunion of Odysseus and Penelope. In *Essays on the Odyssey*, ed. C. Taylor, 100–121. Bloomington: University of Indiana Press.

Anderson, W. S. 1958. Calypso and Elysium. *Classical Journal* 54:2–11.

Austin, N. 1972. Name Magic in the *Odyssey*. *California Studies in Classical Philology* 5:1–19.

Austin, N. 1975. *Archery at the Dark of the Moon*. Berkeley: University of California Press.

Bassi, K. 1999. *Nostos, Domos,* and the Architecture of the Ancient Stage. *South Atlantic Quarterly* 98:415–49.

Bergren, A. 1983. Language and the Female in Early Greek Thought. *Arethusa* 16:69–95.

Beye, C. 1966. *The Iliad, the Odyssey, and the Epic Tradition*. Garden City: Anchor Books.

Beye, C. 1987. *Ancient Greek Literature and Society*. 2nd ed. Ithaca and London: Cornell University Press.

Bradley, E. 1976. The Greatness of His Nature: Fire and Justice in the *Odyssey*. *Ramus* 5:137–48.

Brown, N. O. 1947. *Hermes the Thief*. Madison: University of Wisconsin Press.

Buchan, M. 2004. *The Limits of Heroism*. Ann Arbor: University of Michigan Press.

Burnett, A. 1970. Pentheus and Dionysus: Host and Guest. *Classical Philology* 65:15–29.

Byre, C. 1988. Penelope and the Suitors before Odysseus. *American Journal of Philology* 109:159–73.

Calhoun, G. 1934. Télémaque et le plan de l'Odyssée. *Revue des Études Greques* 47:153–63.

Calhoun, G. 1993. *Ancient Epic Poetry: Homer, Apollonius, Virgil*. Ithaca: Cornell University Press.

Carson, A. 1990. Putting Her in Her Place: Women, Dirt, and Desire. In *Before Sexuality: The Construction of Erotic Experience in the Ancient World*, ed. D. Halperin, J. Winkler, and F. Zeitlin, 135–69. Princeton: Princeton University Press.

Clarke, H. 1963. Telemachus and the *Telemachia*. *American Journal of Philology* 84:129–45.

Clarke, H. 1981. *Homer's Readers: A Historical Introduction to the Iliad and the Odyssey*. Newark: University of Delaware Press.

Clay, J. 1983. *The Wrath of Athena: Gods and Men in the Odyssey*. Princeton: Princeton University Press.

Dimock, G. 1956. The Name of Odysseus. *Hudson Review* 9:52–70.

Dimock, G. 1970. Crime and Punishment in the *Odyssey*. *Yale Review* 50:199–214.

Dimock, G. 1989. *The Unity of the Odyssey*. Amherst: University of Massachusetts Press.

Doherty, L. 1995. *Siren Songs: Gender, Audiences, and Narrators in the Odyssey*. Ann Arbor: University of Michigan Press.

Doherty, L. 2002. The Narrative "Openings" in the *Odyssey*. *Arethusa* 35:51–62.

Edwards, A. 1993. Homer's Ethical Geography: Country and City in the *Odyssey*. *Transactions of the American Philological Association* 123:27–78.

Edwards, M. 1975. Type-Scenes and Homeric Hospitality. *Transactions of the American Philological Association* 105:51–72.

Edwards, M. 1987. *Homer, Poet of the Iliad*. Baltimore: Johns Hopkins University Press.

Emlyn-Jones, C. 1984. The Reunion of Odysseus and Penelope. *Greece and Rome* 31:1–18.

Felson, N. 1997. *Regarding Penelope*. 2nd ed. Norman and London: University of Oklahoma Press.

Fenik, B. 1974. *Studies in the Odyssey*. Hermes Einzelschriften 30. Wiesbaden: F. Steiner.

Finkelberg, M. 1991. Royal Succession in Heroic Greece. *Classical Quarterly* 41:303–16.

Finley, J. 1978. *Homer's "Odyssey."* Cambridge: Harvard University Press.

Finley, M. I. 1978. *The World of Odysseus*. London: Harmondsworth.

Foley, H. 1978. "Reverse Similes" and Sex Roles in the *Odyssey*. *Arethusa* 11:6–26.

Frederiksmeyer, H. 1997. Penelope Polutropos: The Crux at *Odyssey* 23, 218–24. *American Journal of Philology* 118:487–97.

Friedrich, R. 1987. Thrinakia and Zeus' Ways to Men in the *Odyssey*. *Greek, Roman, and Byzantine Studies* 28:375–400.

Gergen, K. 1991. *The Saturated Self: Dilemmas of Identity in Contemporary Life*. New York: Basic Books.

Glenn, J. 1971. The Polyphemus Folktale and Homer's Kyklopeia. *Transactions of the American Philological Association* 102:133–81.

Gregory, E. 1996. Unravelling Penelope. *Helios* 23.1:1–19.

Gross, N. 1976. Nausicaa: A Feminine Threat. *Classical World* 69:311–17.

Hölscher, U. 1939. *Untersuchungen zur Form der Odyssee*. Hermes Einzelscriften 6. Wiesbaden: F. Steiner.

Hölscher, U. 1989. *Die Odyssee: Epos zwischen Märchen und Roman.* Munich: C. H. Beck.

Hyde, L. 1998. *Trickster Makes This World.* New York: Farrar, Straus and Giroux.

Joyce, J. 1986. *Ulysses.* New York: Vintage.

Katz, M. 1991. *Penelope's Renown: Meaning and Indeterminacy in the Odyssey.* Princeton: Princeton University Press.

Kearns, E. 1982. The Return of Odysscus: A Homeric Theoxeny. *Classical Quarterly* 32:2–8.

Kermode, F. 1979. *The Genesis of Secrecy: On the Interpretation of Narrative.* Cambridge: Harvard University Press.

Kirk, G. S. 1962. *The Songs of Homer.* Cambridge: Cambridge University Press.

Lateiner, D. 1992. Heroic Proxemics: Social Space and Distance in the *Odyssey. Transactions of the American Philological Association* 122:133–63.

Lateiner, D. 1993. The Suitors Take: Manners and Power in Ithaca. *Colby Quarterly* 29:172–96.

Levine, D. 1983. Penelope's Laugh: *Odyssey* 18.163. *American Journal of Philology* 104:172–77.

Levy, H. 1963. The Odyssean Suitors and the Host-Guest Relationship. *Transactions of the American Philological Association* 94:145–53.

Lowenstam, S. 2000. The Shroud of Laertes and Penelope's Guilt. *Classical Journal* 95:333–48.

Mackie, H. 1997. Song and Storytelling: An Odyssean Perspective. *Transactions of the American Philological Association* 127:77–95.

Marquand, P. 1985. Penelope polutropos. *American Journal of Philology* 106:32–48.

Martin, R. 1989. *The Language of Heroes: Speech and Performance in the Iliad.* Ithaca: Cornell University Press.

Merton, T. 1958. *Thoughts in Solitude.* New York: Farrar, Straus and Giroux.

Merton, T. 1967. *The Selected Poems of Thomas Merton.* New York: New Directions.

Mondi, R. 1983. The Homeric Cyclopes: Folktale, Tradition, and Theme. *Transactions of the American Philological Association* 113:17–38.

Morgan, K. 1991. *Odyssey* 23.218–24: Adultery, Shame, and Marriage. *American Journal of Philology* 112:1–3.

Most, G. 1989. The Structure and Function of Odysseus' Apologoi. *Transactions of the American Philological Association* 119:15–30.

Murnaghan, S. 1986. Penelope's Agnoia: Knowledge, Power, and Gender in the *Odyssey. Helios* 13:103–15.

Murnaghan, S. 1987. *Disguise and Recognition in the Odyssey.* Princeton: Princeton University Press.

Murnaghan, S. 1995. The Plan of Athena. In *The Distaff Side,* ed. B. Cohen, 61–80. New York: Oxford University Press.

Nagler, M. 1974. *Spontaneity and Tradition: A Study in the Oral Art of Homer.* Berkeley: University of California Press.

Nagler, M. 1977. Dread Goddess Endowed with Speech. *Archaeological News* 6:77–85.

Nagler, M. 1990. The Proem and the Problem. *Classical Antiquity* 9.2:335–56.

Nagy, G. 1979. *The Best of the Achaeans*. Baltimore: Johns Hopkins University Press.

Nagy, G. 1990. *Greek Mythology and Poetics*. Ithaca: Cornell University Press.

Newton, R. 1983. Poor Polyphemus: Emotional Ambivalence in *Odyssey* 9 and 17. *Classical World* 76:137–42.

Oates. J. C. 1999. After Amnesia. In *The Best American Essays, 1999*. New York: Houghton Mifflin, 188–200.

Olson, S. D. 1989. The Stories of Helen and Menelaus (*Od.* 4.240–89) and the Return of Odysseus. *American Journal of Philology* 110:387–94.

Olson, S. D. 1990. The Stories of Agamemnon in Homer's *Odyssey*. *Transactions of the American Philological Association* 120:57–72.

Page, D. 1955. *The Homeric Odyssey*. Oxford: Oxford University Press.

Pantelia, M. 1993. Spinning and Weaving: Ideas of Domestic Order in Homer. *American Journal of Philology* 114:493–500.

Pedrick, V. 1988. The Hospitality of Noble Women in the *Odyssey*. *Helios* 15.2:85–104.

Peradotto, J. 1990. *The Man in the Middle: Name and Narration in Homer's Odyssey*. Princeton: Princeton University Press.

Pucci, P. 1979. The Song of the Sirens. *Arethusa* 12:121–32.

Pucci, P. 1987. *Odysseus Polytropos: Intertextual Readings of the Odyssey and the Iliad*. Ithaca: Cornell University Press.

Reece, S. 1993. *The Stranger's Welcome: Oral Theory and the Aesthetics of the Homeric Hospitality Scene*. Ann Arbor: University of Michigan Press.

Reinhardt, K. 1960. *Tradition und Geist: Gesammelte Essays zur Dictung*. Ed. C. Becker. Göttingen: Vandenhoeck and Ruprecht.

Roisman, H. 1987. Penelope's Indignation. *Transactions of the American Philological Association* 117:59–68.

Rose, G. 1967. The Quest of Telemachus. *Transactions of the American Philological Association* 98:391–98.

Rose, G. 1969. The Unfriendly Phaeacians. *Transactions of the American Philological Association* 100:387–406.

Rose, P. 1992. *Sons of the Gods, Children of Earth*. Ithaca: Cornell University Press.

Russo, J. 1966. The Structural Formula in Homeric Verse. *Yale Classical Studies* 20:219–40.

Russo, J. 1982. "Interview and Aftermath: Dream, Fantasy, and Intuition in *Odyssey* 19 and 20. *American Journal of Philology* 103:4–18.

Russo, J. 1997. A Jungian Analysis of Homer's Odysseus. In *The Cambridge Companion to Jung*, ed. T. Dawson and P. Young-Eisendrath. Cambridge: Cambridge University Press.

Russo, J., M. Fernandez-Galiano, and A. Heubeck. 1992. *A Commentary on Homer's Odyssey: Books XVII–XXIV*. Vol. 3. Oxford: Oxford University Press.

Rutherford, B. 1986. The Philosophy of the *Odyssey*. *Journal of Hellenic Studies* 106:145–62.

Schaeffer, J. 1949. *Shane*. Boston: Houghton Mifflin.

Schein, S. 1970. Odysseus and Polyphemus in the *Odyssey*. *Greek, Roman, and Byzantine Studies* 11:73–83.

Scodel, R. 1998. Bardic Performance and Oral Tradition in Homer. *American Journal of Philology* 119:171–94.

Scully, S. 1987. Doubling in the Tale of Odysseus. *Classical World* 80:401–17.

Segal, C. 1962. The Phaeacians and the Symbolism of Odysseus' Return. *Arion* 1:17–64.

Segal, C. 1992. Divine Justice in the *Odyssey:* Poseidon, Cyclops, and Helios. *American Journal of Philology* 113:489–518.

Snyder, J. 1981. The Web of Song: Weaving Imagery in Homer and the Lyric Poets. *Classical Journal* 76:192–98.

Stanford, W. B. 1958. *The Odyssey of Homer.* Vols. 1–2. London: St. Martin's Press.

Stanford, W. B. 1963. *The Ulysses Theme: Studies in the Adaptability of an Untraditional Hero.* 2nd ed. London: Basil Blackwell.

Stewart, D. 1976. *The Disguised Guest: Rank, Role, and Identity in the Odyssey.* Lewisburg, PA: Bucknell University Press.

Thalmann, W. 1984. *Conventions of Form and Thought in Early Greek Poetry.* Baltimore: Johns Hopkins University Press.

Thalmann, W. 1998. *The Swineherd and the Bow: Representations of Class in the Odyssey.* Ithaca: Cornell University Press.

Tracy, S. 1990. *The Story of the Odyssey.* Princeton: Princeton University Press.

Van Nortwick, T. 1979. Penelope and Nausicaa. *Transactions of the American Philological Association* 109:269–76.

Van Nortwick, T. 1980. *Apollonos Apate:* Associative Imagery in the Homeric *Hymn to Hermes* 227–292. *Classical World* 74:1–5.

Van Nortwick, T. 1992. *Somewhere I Have Never Travelled: The Second Self and the Hero's Journey in Ancient Epic.* New York: Oxford University Press.

Van Nortwick, T. 1998. *Oedipus: The Meaning of a Masculine Life.* Norman: University of Oklahoma Press.

Van Nortwick, T. 2001. Like a Woman: Hector and Boundaries of Masculinity. *Arethusa* 34:221–35.

van Wees, H. 2002. Homer and Early Greece. *Colby Quarterly* 38:94–117.

Webber, A. 1989. The Hero Tells His Name: Formula and Variation in the Phaeacian Episode of the *Odyssey. Transactions of the American Philological Association* 119:1–13.

Wender, D. 1978. *The Last Scenes of the Odyssey.* Mnemosyne Supplement 52. Leiden: Brill.

Whitman, C. 1958. *Homer and the Heroic Tradition.* Cambridge: Harvard University Press.

Winkler, J. 1990. *The Constraints of Desire: The Anthropology of Sex and Gender in Ancient Greece.* London: Routledge.

Wohl, V. 1993. Standing by the Stathmos: The Creation of Sexual Ideology in the *Odyssey. Arethusa* 26:19–46.

Scodel, R. 1994. Hards Performance and Oral Tradition in Homer. *American Journal of Philology* 119:171–94.

Scully, S. 1987. Doublets in the Iliad. *Classical Antiquity* ...

Segal, C. 1994. The Place of the Dead and the Symbolism of Odyssean Return. ... 171–205.

Segal, C. 2001. Divine Justice in the Odyssey: Poseidon, Cyclops, and Helios. *American Journal of Philology* 123:299–38.

INDEX

Achilles: as foil to Odysseus, 59, 115; and Priam, 63–64, 87, 102; in the underworld, 59–60

Aegisthus: as lacking self-control, 6

Aeneas, 18

Agamemnon: as foil to Odysseus, 115; in Hades, 61

Ajax, 60

Alcinous, 49

ambrosia: as sign of deception, 14

Amphinomos, 101–3

animals: as foil for human society, 69

anonymity: as beneficial to hero, 30, 45, 63, 118–19; as conducive to friendship, 73–74, 103; as death, vii, 30, 63; and *kleos*, 45, 62, 64, 103; as liberating, 124–25; of Odysseus, 30, 45

Antikleia, 60, 117

Aphrodite, 87

Apollo: cattle of, 85, 88, 89; duped by Hermes, 89–90; and Pytho, 50

Ares, 87

Arete, 48

Argos (Odysseus' dog), 69

art: role of in human life, 74, 77

Artemis, 109

Athena: as artist, 29, 35, 77, 122; her disguising of Odysseus, 29; as maternal, 22; as orchestrator of return plot, ix, 12, 34, 35, 37, 39, 46, 68, 77, 95, 102, 104, 113, 114, 117; parallel to Calypso, 22; as protector of Odysseus, ix, 5, 12, 22, 34–35, 66–68

Autolycus, 83, 88

Bassi, Karen, 58

bathing: as threatening to hero, 27, 38, 101

Calypso: compared to Circe, 53–55; as dangerous, 14–15; as detaining woman, 17, 20, 100; as emotionally accessible, 16–17; as liminal, 14; her name, 15; Odysseus and, 12–19, 78–79, 90–91; as singer, 14

cattle of the sun, 61–62

Cicones, 49, 117

Circe: as allegorical, 56; compared to Calypso, 53–55; compared to Penelope, 57; as dangerous to Odysseus, 54–55; as detaining woman, 17, 100; as emasculating, 55; episode as comic, 56; episode as microcosm of return plot, 56; Odysseus and 53–57; as surrogate for Athena, 56

Printed and bound by CPI Group (UK) Ltd, Croydon, CR0 4YY

13/04/2025

14656854-0001